30 YEARS

Of DREAMS VISIONS TRANCES

David A. Castro

30 Years of Dreams Visions Trances

Published by: *David A. Castro* Brooklyn, New York
www.brooklynblessing.com   www.twitter.com/daword

Purchase online from: www.Amazon.com

Unless otherwise indicated, Scripture quotations are from *The Holy Bible, King James Version*. Scripture quotations marked "(amp)" are taken from *The Amplified New Testament,* Copyright © 1954, 1958, 1987, by the Lockman Foundation. Used by permission.

Printed in the United States of America

International Standard Book Number: 0-9637001-6-2

TABLE OF CONTENTS

Chapter 1: SHEKINAH GLORY

The Spirit of God can act and behave in any number of ways, both inside of us, and outside of us. Whether in the past or in the present, in any era, God knows everything, can do anything, and is everywhere. He is everywhere, but not in the same way; He is distinctly in some places while in others peculiarly "not there." When He is especially "there" His presence can be considered dwelling in, resting on, or filling that person, place, or thing. God's presence dwelt among the Israelites: the glory filled the temple; the cloud was on Mount Sinai; believers were filled with the Holy Ghost.

The parallels in the Old and New Testaments reveal that God can show up and dwell in a place more especially than in another. In my previous books I go into much more depth on the various kinds of manifestations of the holy presences, so I won't elaborate again here. For our purpose, the current references to the Shekinah—which simply means the presence resting or abiding, (Exodus 40:35)—will be limited to specific, supernatural visitations of the Lord as a cloud that changes the atmosphere of the immediate location, as the Lord does something special.

In thirty years of walking with the Lord, it should not be surprising that I've seen a few silly things in a number of churches. If I was too kind and naïve to indict fools, God Himself would have to tell me things like, "You should be glad you don't have anything to do with those people," (referring to a particular ministry), and, "I don't like them; I don't like what they did to you," (referring to a couple of religious individuals). In a number of different places, I saw such selfishness that I would complain against them and, in one instance, invoked very God. It was April 2006, and the presence that filled my room was such that our very sun could not compare. My whole room was lit up with GOD.

In this visitation, He didn't speak or show visions. He simply rested there. But when I got up and shared it with my Mom, everything that had been on my mind was confirmed with perfect confidence. I already knew that I was correct in my assessments and conclusions about certain religious leaders—because I knew the details in reality and because of other episodes of spiritual discernment—but to have God so fully affirm them brought me to an even more sure place. GOD in my room!

If I was not already in a place with God that I didn't need people trying to lay hands on me and anoint me and impart something to me so that I would have more of God, I certainly was from then on. (I don't know what gets into people that they quickly take confidence to lay hands on folks.) While I was telling Mom about God being in our home in a distinctive way on that occasion, I boldly asserted that if one hundred of the most anointed, powerful, gifted men and women of God were to line up so each one could lay hands on me and pray and impart some anointing to me, I would decline. That's how much God came into the room: even a thousand prophets cannot compare to Him! He later told me to throw out the anointing oil that I'd been using when I pray. I hesitated for a few days, but eventually threw it out.

The day after the visitation, I shared it with 2 friends of mine, ministers, and they listened intensely, staring and not saying a word. They thanked God. Glorious things do indeed occur among God's people in a number of churches and ministries, and there are many Holy Spirit-filled individuals upon whom the anointing rests in distinctive, extraordinary ways. Although He may work in a great variety of ways (and not always as a fire and smoke that everyone will see), it is the same Shekinah Glory of God that rests on His chosen people.

Around summertime 1988, I was riding a Greyhound bus on my way to one of Rev. Kenneth Copeland's conferences, in Fort Worth, Texas, at the Tarrant County Convention Center. While on the highway, some time after midnight, I became keenly aware of the presence of God inside like a fog. As I looked at the passengers, they all appeared to be not just resting, but in a veritable *deep sleep from the Lord.* They seemed to have been overcome by the weighty presence of the Lord. I looked at the driver's face (I was sitting in the front passenger seat) and he, too, looked like he was in a trance, just staring at the road in front of him.

At that time of morning on Greyhound buses it was usual to find someone reading, eating, listening to music or talking with other passengers, and the driver might have had a portable radio on. Often people sleep during the day while on long road trips on the buses and the nighttime can be quite lively. I know because I have traveled on these buses many times. But this time there was absolutely no movement, activity or sound. I just looked over to the passengers with amazement at how still they all were, and got a lesson on how people look when they are in a deep sleep from the Lord.

Also, one would usually be able to hear the sound of the wheels going over the road and rocks and pebbles being flung every few seconds—but not then. I searched for the sound of the wheels on the road, the motor on the bus or the wind against the windows—but nothing. I stared for about a minute at the driver, and he just wouldn't budge. A great eighteen-wheeler drove slowly by us on the right side, on my side of the bus, so I looked up to see its driver and, lo and behold, he, too, appeared to be in a stupor or trance. He didn't look down to see the bus (he didn't look around at all), didn't have a natural expression on his face, and didn't honk his horn even once. I thought he would probably turn his head a bit and see me, but no; he looked just like the bus driver: in a stupor from the Lord.

As I looked at the large wheels of the truck roll by me, I searched for the sound of them going over the road and flinging rocks and pebbles. But there was no sound; there was nothing but complete, divine silence. Again, I was keenly aware of the fact that the Shekinah Glory of God—although He didn't give me a message—was traveling with me on that bus. I knew that God was there in a supernatural way, albeit, perhaps, for no particular reason. This presence was noticeable for about ten or fifteen minutes, to the best of my recollection. Then the thin vapor of smoke faded away, and I was able to notice everone and everything normalizing: the motor, sounds of wheels outside and flinging pebbles, driver and passengers moving about and beginning to chat.

Around 1997, I had a visitation of the glory cloud in my room, as I was half awake and half asleep in a trance. I saw a brilliant cloud with flashing lights, and with many small lightning bolts coming out of it. I started saying to myself, "God is here. God is here." God spoke to me but I couldn't understand His words. The presence was so terrifying I thought I might die. I felt as if, inwardly, my jaw fell open in awesome fear and my eyes popped open and stuck out of their sockets in dread of what I was seeing. In the famous cartoon "Casper, the friendly ghost," when people saw Casper and got scared, their jaws dropped all the way down to the floor and their eyes springed several inches out of their sockets, and that's exactly the way I felt in that presence. It seemed I was totally found out and undone, and had nowhere to go to hide, His consuming fire and holy presence was so evident. "There shall no man see Me, and live," (Exodus 33.20). Even though I felt amazingly frightened, He didn't come to consume or punish me.

Then He told me to read some of the many statements He'd written on my window shade, in the spiritual realm. I could only remember one. It said, "Pray for Mom's checkbook." The most I can understand from this sovereign visitation of God (and I don't use the word "sovereign" lightly) is that in some lives He Himself is going to show up in our finances and glorify Himself sovereignly. In my case, since He had called me aside to hang out with Him for a couple of decades, His provision came through Mom. A few days later, my mother received an unexpected check in the mail for several hundred dollars. I wasn't able to catch the seven or eight other things God had written spiritually on my shade, but He is going to accomplish those things, too. (In 1992, in an out-of-body experience, Jesus had spoken to me audibly, saying,

"I always hold back My things for an hour.")

The scary presence of flashing lights, lightning bolts, and a terror of the Lord being in my room, I have come to understand to mean that He was angry that He was being forced to redesign my life's circumstances. Events in my life were such that there was no way out of the constricted condition, and He, unscripted as it were, came gloriously to re-write the script and dwell in that which was not His original plan for me.

I attended Drake Business School from July 1999 to March 2000 and graduated with honors that month. My experience there was enjoyable and memorable, and got me inspired to go to college over the next few years. But I did have some problems. A handful of foolish persons brought some persecution my way and tried to make my time there impossible; they got me on probation just within three weeks of the beginning of my program, almost got me kicked out, threatened to have me beaten up, and one even brought her husband to deal with me. He took one look at me and left.

During my last term, while doing a research paper on "The Current Visitation of God in the Earth," I happened to be alone in my classroom; for some strange reason, my three classmates and the instructor all had other engagements for that hour. Each day of class there would always be all kinds of noises and sounds throughout the school: instructors teaching, students talking and typing on keyboards, books and papers shuffling, phones ringing from the administrative offices, people walking through the hallway, and the sounds of traffic and people heard coming through the windows. The school was located on the busy intersection of Broadway and Steinway Street in Astoria, New York, a commercial district; the classroom was on the third floor, and it was during the early afternoon of a weekday. Naturally, there was always a lot of activity and noise in the atmosphere—but not on that day.

For about a twenty minute period of time, as I looked at the computer screen and began writing the research paper, and thought about the current move of

God, (and particularly the *Toronto Blessing*), the Shekinah Glory Cloud of God visited me in that room. He had arranged for me to be alone so that He can be with *me*. I didn't fall into a trance, hadn't dozed off and had a daydream, and wasn't simply imagining the presence of the Holy Spirit: I was fully awake and in my right mind, knew where I was and what was around me, and knew that it was the Shekinah Glory literally there.

I was keenly aware of the absence of sounds—no phones ringing, no people or traffic heard coming from the windows, no one walking through the hallway, no one typing, talking or teaching, even though all the other classrooms were filled with students and instructors and computers. It was not simply a rarity but a natural impossibility that at such a time of day, at such a place, there would be absolutely no movement or speech for as long as twenty minutes. And, as usual, the classroom doors were open. God had come into the building and entranced the whole of it, and I knew it. It was clear to me that every individual in that building was in a similar stupor as all those on that floor, and maybe anyone in the vicinity outside, too, because there was absolutely no activity inside or outside.

I said, "God, You're here. You're here. Your Shekinah Glory is literally right here, right now, and I know it. Why are You here, Lord? Is there a special reason for Your glory being here this way?" He put thoughts in my mind that I translate: "I'm affirming what you're writing about because I'm truly in it," (the global move of God that was influenced by the *Toronto Blessing*, beginning in 1994) and "I'm blessing you for obeying Me in coming to this school and toughing it out, and I'm delivering you from the vexation placed on you by those who persecuted you."

All through the time of His presence there was such a holy silence in the atmosphere that one could hear a pin drop. I was very aware of the fact that God had put everyone in that building in a *deep sleep from the Lord*—as he did to King Saul's soldiers when the Psalmist David penetrated Saul's guard and captured his spear and cruse of water, (1Samuel 26:12)—and left them with absolutely no knowledge of the event. But I knew it and have kept it as precious all these years. When the Shekinah lifted and faded away, sounds, talking and activity gradually resumed as normal and I enjoyed an otherwise normal day.

God can do glorious things right in the middle of regular, normal activities without anyone knowing about it. The fools who sought to trouble me quit the program and didn't graduate. Three years later, the school (which had been in business for over a hundred years), in all its locations, went bankrupt and is no longer in business.

I earned the Computerized Business certificate from Drake Business School in 2000, and also the Perfect Attendance and Outstanding Mentor and Dean's List awards. The experience was wholly rewarding, and I have remained close friends with some of my graduating classmates: Phillip, Andrea, Jorge and Cristina. Somehow, they still consider me their mentor a decade later. We have all grown spiritually, visited church together, and accomplished what we set out to do while at Drake.

I went on to earn an Associate in Applied Sciences degree in Digital Media Communications from The Katharine Gibbs School in 2003, and a Bachelor of Science degree in Media Studies from the State University of New York's Empire State College in 2005. In the spring of 2004, I was already looking into the possibility of further studies and graduate programs.

The Lord spoke to me about one of the schools I started considering. I thought it offered a great program, but one morning I heard the Lord say, "PANDORA'S BOX," as if in capital letters. I was certain He was referring to that particular school, so I didn't apply. But I shared the revelation with a couple of my friends that attended there, and they were not surprised. When I shared it with one while accompanying her home on a train, a unique event occurred. I stood in front of PhAnie sharing the Voice in an animated tone (usual for me) and, as if inspired, I turned around and looked behind me and noticed a lady sitting and reading a book. I leaned over to see the cover (also usual for me) and it read "PANDORA'S BOX!" (It is a story about a treasure chest containing evil.)

Astoundedly, I told PhAnie and she was amazed, too. How telling, and how undeniable, was that message. God was letting me know that something bad was contained in that school, and led me elsewhere.

I applied to City University of New York's Brooklyn College, and enjoyed God's blessing in the Master of Arts in Liberal Studies program, from which I graduated in 2007. Initially in the program in the spring 2005, I almost transferred to Brooklyn College's new PIMA program (Performance and Interactive Media Arts) because it merged curricula from several traditional and new media production programs, something I am very interested in. But in a trance with the glory of God in manifestation, the Lord revealed to me, "You should stay in Liberal Studies." I instantly voided my transfer application and completed the Liberal Studies program, and got a lot out of it.

Having written a thesis on new media technology and its influence on the entertainment industry, I came across a number of writers that stressed the importance of a liberal arts education for those interested in making movies and other artistic texts. They encouraged students to learn about life and human nature and the social sciences more than about production techniques. Obviously, I praised God for leading me to do exactly that—instead of production—even before I realized the importance of the liberal arts. I have thanked Him a thousand times for opening the door for me to study at Brooklyn College, which is considered "Brooklyn's Harvard."

Having completed that program, my Media Studies program at The New School University, which included a lot of production techniques, and from which I graduated in 2008, became all the more enriching, and proved the apex of my awesome educational journey (my back-to-college-in-middle-age experience). If I can explain why God has blessed me as much as He has in my College Drop-In decade, I'm sure it is in large part because of my honorable attitude. I have counted as gold every part of all the schools I have attended, and even those I didn't enroll in. I have held in high regard all my professors and school administrators, and have shown respect and appreciation for the resources available to me: the buildings, classrooms, libraries, and computer labs. And I have offered to assist anyone I can with anything, if it was in my power. The reward of His smile is more than I can describe, and I'm a man of many words.

Before going back to school in 1999, I had done some traveling around the nation and networking with Christian ministries. In 1994, during a prophetic conference in West Haven, Connecticut, I stayed in the home of Pastor Brian Simmons, and dreamed that someone said to me, "You ought to move to New England." As soon as he said that, a wind came through the closed window and shook the house, and startled me as it woke me. I knew it was literal, and thought I'd share that with Brian later. When he caught up to me later that day, he excitedly related that he had heard and felt a wind that blew through the window and shook the house and startled him, waking him up. We both agreed it occurred at the exact same time, nearly 6:00 a.m. "What was that about?" Brian asked. I said, "God is going to do *something* when David A. Castro comes to New England."

Fifteen years later, nothing has come of that visitation of Shekinah, however, a few dreams in 2008 assure me that that word has not fallen to the ground.

Praying before going to Connecticut to minister, sometime in 1998, I saw a vision of an angel (Gabriel, I think) blowing a trumpet and going ahead of me and hovering over the church. I had a strong sense of an apostolic anointing; and I saw a river and its name "Connecticut River." I didn't even know that there was a river in Connecticut, much less that that was its name, but one of the administrators confirmed that it is so, and that it lies just a short distance from the church I was to minister in, in the city of Windsor Locks.

Though it was invisible, an apostolic anointing, assisted by the ministry of the archangel Gabriel, was present in the ministry there, during which I spoke on the important theme of "How God Speaks."

House-sitting in Kansas City for James W. Goll in 1992, I was laying on the living room floor one morning. In a trance, my eyes were opened and I saw the hem of an angel's robe garment and it had bells like the priests' in the Old Testament and he was burning incense as they did back then. This confirmed the spiritual reality of James' priestly disposition—which confirmation I didn't need—because, being a prophetic intercessor, he is anointed to minister as those priests of old.

My stepdad was working in my room one day and couldn't stay. He said he could not endure God's presence there. Many of my dreams and visions over the years have featured glorious lights and heavenly sounds, as of angels. By His numerous visitations, God has chosen to dwell here, permitted me to be aware of His presence and, further, to help others understand some of the workings of His dynamic presence.

Everyone that knows me knows that God uses me in dream interpretation, but no one has ever discerned or prophetically revealed to me that my ancestors were Jewish. When I shared with someone that my family is Sephardic, she said, "Oh, no wonder you have an anointing like the prophets of old, like Daniel and Joseph." Even though God can distinguish anyone from any background with a special anointing, it makes sense that this is given to someone related to Israel, whom God called His chosen people.

When I would see Messianic Jews teaching and sharing in the churches, I secretly was jealous because, even though God gave me spiritual blessings every time I asked, they had the distinction of being God's chosen people, and that was something that God could not simply create for me by changing my nationality. He could not change where I come from. I was Puerto Rican, and nothing could really change that. So, as much as I could be blessed spiritually, I would always be Puerto Rican, however proud. Then one day in May 2002, I dreamed that I was in Israel being honored by Jewish leaders. I was becoming Jewish and my skin was turning bronze. I woke up thinking, "But I'm Puerto Rican. This must simply mean that I am Jewish "spiritually," as all Christians are, according to the Apostle Paul," (Romans 2:29). However, it seemed real.

That evening, my cousin George Vazquez (who only calls about once a year) called to relate his newfound insight on the Sephardic history of our family. Being affiliated with Messianic Christians for four decades, he had studied and discovered that all the last names among our family members are the most likely to be directly or indirectly connected to those families that crossed the Atlantic from Spain (such as my great great grandmother), many of whom were Israelites fleeing persecution and adopting Spanish culture and names.

What a tremendous confirmation; it has upgraded my understanding of many things. When I shared this revelation with an administrator from a Jewish Theological Seminary, she chuckled at my excitement. "We hear reports like this very often," she said. "God never ceases to amaze me," I said, "because He did what I thought He could not do: by connecting my family to Spain and Israel, He made me an Israelite! And I'm still Puerto Rican and proud!"

Now more then ever, it makes sense to me why He would show up in our home the way He does, with the Shekinah Glory in manifestation as it was among the Israelites over several millennia: not only because He likes Latin sabor and passion, but because we are His chosen people, too.

THE OUTPOURING OF THE HOLY SPIRIT

The variety and levels of intensity of the manifest anointing is exhorbitant and cannot easily be categorized. A powerful manifestation of the Holy Spirit is not necessarily the Shekinah Glory, and neither is a great city-wide or nation-wide revival. Nevertheless, we can experience many glorious presences of God that stand out, that are distinctive.

What is distinctive? I used to think a *revival of the Holy Spirit,* or an *outpouring of the Spirit,* or a *supernatural manifestation,* or a *move of God,* was necessarily noisy and dynamic, with visual evidences of God doing stuff. In Pentecostal tradition, this is what those have been.

When we see a lot of dynamic activity in a revival service, such as people speaking with other tongues, falling under the power of God, and being healed, we like to say, *"This is that,* which was spoken by the prophet Joel," (Acts 2:16), which is to say that there is [necessarily] dynamic activity when the Spirit is poured out. This can, indeed, be true because when the Spirit comes and touches flesh, flesh yields in some way. And the Bible does, in fact, say, "The voice of rejoicing and salvation is in the tabernacles of the righteous," (Psalms 118:15). But this definition has been upgraded in my thinking lately. Here's another take on the event:

"Peace be unto you," Jesus said, (John 20:19), while standing right there in the midst of the disciples. "Be still, and know that I am God" sings the psalmist, (Psalms 46:10). Stillness and peace, as a manifestation of a move of God in the midst, can be a collective experience, just as it often is an individual experience. A mind in turmoil—characterized by rampant thoughts, confusion, lunacy and panic—can experience perfect peace and normal thinking when Jesus says to it, "Peace, be still." A whole church community, city, or nation, can also be brought to a state of peace, harmony, and normalcy, as God covers it with His presence.

Rev. Kenneth E. Hagin said that during a totally still and silent church service (over sixty years ago), an unbeliever came in and sat. No one moved or said a word. After awhile, the individual felt the conviction to dedicate his life to the Lord; he stood up, made his way to the altar trembling, and got gloriously saved. He accepted Jesus as his Savior and spoke in tongues, without anyone's assistance. Nowadays we are too quick to jump on people and school them through. But if we would take a chill pill and trust God, we might see more glorious things. God (His anointing, that is) is not all the time in the dynamic human effort, or in the voice of rejoicing and noise.

On January 7, 2009, I dreamed of New York City about 10 or 20 years from then. The Lord's presence was everywhere, the glory of God had taken over the city and it was marvelous. But everything was normal. The city was intact—it had not been destroyed by water or fire or anything—and the normal business of everyday life continued as it is today. People were working, going to school, driving cars, and there were a number of new buildings, and the streets were very clean, calm and safe.

In other city-wide revivals in history, there would be similar manifestations of peace, including significant decrease of crime, and many would be added to the Church daily, as many as the Lord would call. So, as much as some groups love the dynamic activity historically attributed to the Pentecostals, which is noise and movement, let us get ready to embrace the manifestation of the Holy Spirit that may be characterized by other activity, such as calmness, perfect peace, and normal thinking that facilitates the knowledge of the Lord. "For the earth shall be filled with the knowledge of the glory of the Lord, as the waters cover the sea" (Habakkuk 2:14), and the sea can be active or calm.

An officer in the Salvation Army once told me that in her services they often feel as ecstatic as the Pentecostals (who are known for running, jumping, and yelling), yet they remain still, enjoying the various touches of God privately. Many other churches, ministries, and individuals, also experience the ecstasies of God in a number of ways not characteristic of the more animated Pentecostals. I myself was becoming gloriously introduced to the ecstatic realm of visions and revelations even before becoming familiar with those churches and ministries that are lively like the Pentecostals.

I became a Christian in 1979, in Honolulu, Hawaii, and returned to New York

City in the same year, but it was in 1982 that I became a member of a Pentecostal church and started speaking with other tongues. For the first three years of my walking with the Lord, it was mostly just me and the Lord, and the move of His Spirit in my life produced not "Pentecostal manifestations" (except privately), but His move in my life at that time produced peace and repose. I do support and enjoy those manifestations. But we have got to become ecumenical and understand that many will not embrace that doctrine or religion style; yet we have got to embrace them.

John 17:22-23 And the glory which Thou gavest me I have given them; that they may be one, even as We are one: I in them, and Thou in Me, that they may be made perfect in one; and that the world may know that Thou hast sent Me, and hast loved them, as thou hast loved me.

In the move of God that we are in, which is going to become more extensive and world-encompassing, we will have to permit others' theologies if we are going to please Jesus, because His wish is for unity—not doctrinal, but spiritual unity. We've got to not only put up with each other, but, believe that another's journey and religious understanding and spiritual style is valid in the sight of God. They are the Lord's.

In an infomercial on television, there's a spiritual healer that I unfairly disdained and instantly changed channels on whenever I saw him, because his style and statements were unlike mine. He also had religious artifacts and wore a ceremonial headdress and spoke like a guru while praying for the sick in the Name of Jesus. In a dream, the Lord educated me, showing that he was legitimately serving God, even though he did not use the more popular Christian lingo. I had sought to get along with and love everyone, so the Lord was teaching me that grace and acceptance is a part of that. The Apostle Paul echoes the idea in Romans, Chapter 14:

"Him that is weak in the faith receive ye, but not to doubtful disputations. For one believeth that he may eat all things: another, who is weak, eateth herbs. Let not him that eateth despise him that eateth not; and let not him which eateth not judge him that eateth: for God hath received him. Who art thou that judgest another man's servant? To his master he standeth or falleth. Yea, he shall be holden up: for God is able to make him stand. One man esteemeth one day above another: another esteemeth every day alike. Let every man be fully persuaded in his own mind. He that regardeth the day, regardeth it unto the Lord; and he that regardeth not the day, to the Lord he doth not regard it. He that eateth, eateth to the Lord, for he giveth God thanks, and he that eateth not, to the Lord he eateth not, and giveth God thanks," (verses 1-6).

"But why dost thou judge thy brother? Or why dost thou set at nought thy brother? For we shall all stand before the judgment seat of Christ. For it is written, As I live, saith the Lord, every knee shall bow to me, and every tongue shall confess to God. So then every one of us shall give account of himself to God. Let us not therefore judge one another any more: but judge this rather, that no man put a stumblingblock or an occasion to fall in his brother's way. I know, and am persuaded by the Lord Jesus, that there is nothing unclean of itself: but to him that esteemeth any thing to be unclean, to him it is unclean," (verses 10-14).

"For the Kingdom of God is not meat and drink; but righteousness, and peace, and joy in the Holy Ghost. For he that in these things serveth Christ is acceptable to God, and approved of men. Let us therefore follow after the things which make for peace, and things wherewith one may edify another. …All things indeed are pure," (verses 17-20).

1John 4:8 He that loveth not knoweth not God; for God is love.

Chapter 2: FAMILY HISTORY

All my grandparents were from the beautiful island of Puerto Rico. They came to Brooklyn, New York City, to make new lives for themselves. My mother was ill with rickets and it was thought she would die at the age of 3 months. Her father, Frank Vazquez, brought her to a miracle service in the neighborhood where an evangelist from Mexico was preaching the Gospel and praying for the sick. Frank told God, "If You heal my daughter, I will dedicate my life to You and serve you always." God instantly and miraculously healed Mom, and grandfather did serve God all his life, establishing churches and winning souls for Jesus until he died at the age of 84. My other grandfather, Roque Castro, also served God and established several churches. Both my grandmothers were devoted to prayer.

There were several apostolic ministers in my family. Uncle John Vazquez, on my mother's side of the family, was one of the founding members of the International Christian Boy Scouts *The Royal Rangers.* Mom's sister Edith was a Missionary, whose husband, Rev. Ramon Rodriquez, established several churches in Chicago and California, and helped strengthen others in New York and Florida for nearly six decades. Mom's brother, Rev. George Vazquez, (who died when he was only 35) preached and prophesied and often danced and jumped in the Holy Spirit. He also sang and played the accordion, piano, and guitar; he and Mom, who also sang and played the piano and guitar, were a duet. I remember seeing Uncle George drink raw eggs to clear his throat before church services. His son, George Vazquez, Jr., who has been affiliated with Messianic congregations since the 1970's, has always been a passionate minister of the Gospel.

My nephew, Rev. Victor Armando Crespo, III, has also come to carry the Gospel torch in more recent decades.

Mom's difficult marriage resulted in her raising us by herself on welfare. If she worked, my father (who always had money because he managed clothing factories) took her paycheck, beat her up, and lived the high and lewd life. He cursed me wishing I would die in the womb, and threw a knife at Mom's belly while I was still in it, though missing it. They separated when I was one year old, and later divorced. How he turned out as bad as he did, we cannot understand, given his holy parents and religious upbringing.

I am the youngest of four, and we were the poorest family in our building, probably on the block. We didn't have much, but appreciated what little we had. We had each other, and it was fun having activity in the house all the time, with Mom and the four of us. We went to a variety of churches, including Catholic, Baptist, and Pentecostal. One of the most anointed prophetesses in our city, Pastor Colon of Bushwick Avenue, asked Mom often if she could adopt me. She always said, "No." I am so thankful that she did. I like who I am, and I cannot imagine where I would be today if I had been raised differently.

My older sisters, Naomi and Ruth, would talk to me and my brother, Carlos, about God, since they received higher instruction at church. I thought it was fascinating that there was someone up there that sees everything and knows everything and can do anything, and that He loves me. We lived on the fifth floor of a residential building and had to take turns going down to the store and throwing the garbage out, which we all hated doing. There was always talk and play and other activities in the home, but I discovered that in my "alone time" going downstairs to the store or to throw out garbage, I could talk with God. When I stopped complaining about it, but engaged the duties gladly, Mom said, "What are you doing when you go downstairs? You're not supposed to be happy, you were always complaining about it." I told Mom, "I'm talking with God when I go down and have this alone time."

I am thankful for the upbringing with my lively family, and also lots of cousins, uncles and aunts, and energetic immediate community. However, I was not able to have the kind of communication with the Lord that, apparently, has always been there ready to unfold whenever I could yield. Even though there were ministers on both sides of my family that preached to me and prayed for me, I was never convinced about believing in the old-time religion. I needed a personal God that would be my friend—although I didn't know how to articulate that at that time—but I was always directed to religious practice instead of the relationship with God that I was really looking for.

Chapter 3: HOW I BECAME A CHRISTIAN

When I turned 14, I went to a Catholic school in Lincolndale, New York, for a year and a half, and graduated in 1972 with honors as I excelled in academics and in sports, and won a trip to Washington, D.C. I was documented as being one of the very best students that they ever had. But it was because the Lord had spoken clearly to me. Initially, it was very difficult for me being in that school, away from home. I was getting into fights, wasn't making friends, and ran away a few times. But I had been trying to talk to God, and showing Him my painful situation. One day He spoke audibly, "My peace I give to you." I was so startled I thought someone was playing games with me and started looking all over the dormitories and under the beds and in the closets to see who had said that. When I realized it was Jesus, I couldn't contain my excitement. I went to the recreation area, and it seemed the whole world had changed. The boys started making friends with me, I felt I could complete the year-and-a-half long program there, and I did well in everything.

I attended Bushwick High School while living with Mom again in Brooklyn, and I graduated with honors in 1974. However, on graduation day I didn't feel like I got the education I should have gotten. I skipped class a lot and didn't perform as well as I could have. Even so, at home I was always reading nonfiction, since I became interested in psychology and planned to go to college, Stony brook University in Long Island.

While at Stony Brook, which actually was a great experience and turning point for me, I became distracted by the party atmosphere and dropped out in 1976. I was a Wall Street messenger for a while, and then became interested in going to Hawaii, to study Chi Kung and Chinese Philosophy in Aina Haina, a section of Oahu just behind Diamond Head, east of Waikiki. I was there for about nine months, from December 1978 to August 1979.

On my first night in Hawaii, I had to sleep on a beach (since I didn't know anyone there and had only twenty-two bucks in my pocket), but in the morning I saw a man that I believe was an angel watching me as if to protect me.

I was homeless for the first seven weeks of my time there, and went many days without eating, and walking looking for work. I never asked strangers for change, but a couple of church people were generous occasionally. I slept in parks, beaches, empty buildings and construction sights.

Eventually, I found work: at McDonald's, Jack in the Box, the Honolulu Zoo, Dole Pineapple Plant, and Fiddler's Shutter Repair Shop. I made some friends, too, and they loved to talk about Jesus. I did get to start Chi Kung classes, which lasted about four months. I became a Christian, and that changed everything!

While in the Chinese temple alone one day, I started calling upon Jesus to save me from a visitation of a dark spirit, and within about a minute or two, a glorious light appeared and dispelled the darkness, leaving a tremendous sense of divine peace. I knew the presence of Jesus had shown up, and I began to embrace Him as my newfound Lord and Savior. It felt like I was on a heavenly cloud on the bus trip back to Honolulu, where I was living; and that feeling lasted a few days. I began to consider myself a Christian mostly from that day on. I had had a couple of other conversion experiences about that same time, but the one in the temple, in July 1979, was most notable.

On an earlier occasion, I had bought a radio so I could listen to Gospel dialog. When I was little, my Mom and other grownups in the family were listening to Gospel preaching on radio and enjoying it, and I secretly thought that that's something that I myself will do if I ever need spiritual help when I grow up. Now in Hawaii, I was looking for God and got really excited when I found a Christian radio station. Someone was saying, "I saw God, man; I'm telling you I saw God. I was going to get high but He spoke to me and told me He loves me, and I got saved!"

I started wishing that something like that would happen to me, and cried many tears asking God to change and improve my life. There were many times there that I cried out to the Lord asking Him to save me.

I started visiting churches and watching Christian television programs, but I still drank a beer or smoked marijuana occasionally. I don't remember having supernatural experiences during that time, except for one that I did have, which was of a group of people, like a council, observing me, and one of them was rebuking me and threatening to deal harshly with me for not serving God. I couldn't believe that I actually could see and hear them in the air, looking at me and trying to set me straight. The main person was harsh, but the others asked him to be merciful to me and give me another chance at getting my life correctly in line with God's will for me. My life really wasn't bad, since I was working in Hawaii and going to that Chi Kung School. But the Lord had bigger plans, which were not being accommodated.

As it turned out, I did leave Hawaii as a Christian and returned to Brooklyn, and in two days I was offered a full-time career appointment, with all the benefits, in the United States Postal Service. It was during my three and a half years there that I began to establish a close relationship with the Lord and that He began to open the heavens unto me and show me great and mighty things that I knew not. Now that I was twenty-four years old and a new Christian living with Mom, the kind of communication that had waited for me to yield was finally given the chance to begin to unfold.

I remember calling Mom from Hawaii one day and telling her the good news about my epiphany with Jesus. Her dad and siblings, and some of my cousins, had tried unsuccessfully to teach me about Jesus and help me become a Christian. They were all concerned about my odd journey to Hawaii, too. But hearing from Mom that I had found the Lord, by a direct, personal, supernatural encounter (which they, being Pentecostals, thoroughly believed in), they were all so thankful. They knew that if all their preaching could not convert me, but that God Himself had to do it, something unique had to be underway.

I had stopped by Florida and Kansas City before heading out to Hawaii. While in Florida, being preached to and prayed for by Rev. Ramon and Aunt Edith, they wished God's blessing on me and asked God to show me the light. I can only imagine the elation throughout the family when they heard the great news of my salvation. My whole family was convinced I'd had an epiphany, and they realized that God Himself had taken up my life and was beginning to educate me in the things of the Holy Spirit.

Chapter 4: I WANT TO SERVE GOD

If passionately seeking and esteeming the things of God can facilitate an encounter with Him, disdain for evil is consistent with that. Since I was always studious, both in and out of school, I found myself frequenting the New York Public Library on 5th Avenue and 42nd Street, around 1977-78, before going to Hawaii. One day, I somehow found myself in the grand library, which is the second largest in the nation, in a special section for books on parapsychology, the paranormal, and mysticism. In researching psychological themes, these other topics are always found close by. I was intrigued.

I sat alone at a large table with several books I had pulled from the shelves for perusal, reference books that cannot be taken out. A very large, old volume was most interesting; it looked like one of those you'd find in a movie about witches and warlocks, and I thought, "Wow, what a privilege! Does the world know about this? I will surely get something out of this."

I took my time getting ready to peruse it, and began going through the first few pages. I quickly came upon a page that captivated and sobered me. It was a grave warning, so I made sure I read it carefully and completely. In brief, it basically said that there were powers and forces within the pages that followed and that it could potentially prove dangerous. For those that are not ready or that feel uncomfortable with this kind of text, it is better not to open it but close it and put it away.

I may not be a genius, but thank God I'm not stupid. At first I thought I might take the chance and begin looking through the rest of the book, but not without contemplating it for a minute. During that minute, as if influenced, I concluded that I honestly was not ready for that information at all, and thought that I have the opportunity to come back some other time when I am more sure about the inquiry. Somehow, that other time never came. I listened to that still, small influence that cautioned me to heed the warning. Whew!

Still a non-Christian around the same year, I met someone that was talking positively about witchcraft, and I took up his invitation to take part in a prayer with him and someone else. In the dark event, with candles, robes, and incantations, I was asked to read a spell from a paper. As the ceremony seemed to drag on, it seemed someone was speaking to me from between me and the witch (it had to be an angel of God), and was telling me that this is not a good thing for me to do, and that those kinds of activities are hard to recover from once engaged. I was forced to take most seriously the event at hand. The angel finally asked if I wanted to go through with it, and in my mind I answered him, "No. So how do I get out of here?" "Just tell him you decline," I heard, so that's what I did and, thankfully, the host was very civil and understanding.

A newly born-again Christian by the time I started working in the Postal Service, at the Gracie Mansion Post Office on the Upper East Side of Manhattan, I had absolutely resolved to read the Word of God and other edifying books that would enrich my newfound walk with the Lord. It was not long before I started seeing my ceiling open and heavenly revelations disclosed. I had not been studying about dreams, visions, and supernatural revelations, or asking or expecting or otherwise initiating these things, but they just came down. If heaven was holding back all these things until I became a Christian, they seemed to suddenly burst upon me at the fullness of the time, when I resolved to seek the Lord with all my heart.

Since I worked during the night shift at the Post Office, I often heard the regular hustle and bustle of neighborhood activity when just getting ready to go to sleep about 9:00 each morning. Many times, I would sleep with loud noise or music around me, and yet I could clearly hear audible messages from the Lord without hearing any of the exterior sounds. It was like a soundproof shield surrounded me for the duration of the visitation. Without being distracted, I would be able to see the dreams and visions He would reveal. Angels would stop my external ears while communicating to my spiritual ears. Only before and after the messages could I hear the natural sounds.

These kinds of experiences moved me and changed me. I began to walk upon the high places of the earth, which means I was being lifted in my relationship with God and in my self-concept. I started visiting churches and learning Pentecostal doctrine. I became passionate about anything that had to do with God, and began to wish I could become a preacher some day.

I did a lot of praying and fasting. I fasted for thirteen days (drinking juice and water) before receiving the Holy Spirit with the tongues experience, in 1982, while at a conference with Kenneth Copeland Ministries. I had also collected many anointed teaching tapes and books, getting edified with the Word of God as it was taught and preached by ministers who had gotten to places in God that I hoped to arrive at.

Whereas I had thought street preachers and those who give out Gospel pamphlets had no merit, and that they were an eyesore, since becoming a Christian I began to wish that I could be one of them and do what they did. Over time, God prepared me for that and in 1982, I launched out by myself. The first time I did was in the fall of 1982, in Manhattan, and something unique happened.

While preaching from the Bible on East 86th Street, a man came from around the corner and started walking straight toward me. He looked just like Jesus: about six feet tall, hair over the shoulders, and a beard; however, he had modern clothes. I felt uncomfortable since he kept walking straight toward me, even as he crossed the two-way street. I thought I would get into a defensive karate stance if he comes within two feet of me, but for some reason I just kept on preaching when he came up to me, kissed me on the right cheek, and said, "Keep on doing what you're doing." He was bold and resolute in the act, turned around, and walked away, disappearing around the corner on my side of the street. I hadn't stopped preaching in the whole event, or ever since.

About three months later, I resigned from the Postal Service, "To preach the Gospel of the Lord Jesus Christ," which is what I wrote on the official Resignation Form. Beginning January 1983, a new anointing came into my life, as I had become dedicated to seeking the things which are Above, as encouraged by the preachers on tapes and in books, and by the Lord who ignited my passion.

In a church service with the Holy Spirit moving upon Sister Tati, she started walking backward toward me with her eyes closed and speaking with other tongues. She somehow made her way around the many chairs between us, but when she got to me she lifted her hand and I took hold of it so she wouldn't lose her balance. But instead of letting my hand go, she started walking me back up toward the front, where her husband, Pastor Ismael Roman, interpreted what Tati had been speaking with other tongues. The Lord inspired him to say, "This young man wants to serve God." It was one of the confirmations assuring me that I was on the right track.

At the convention center in Tulsa, Oklahoma, during a Bible teaching conference with Kenneth Hagin Ministries in 1983, while lying down outside on the lawn between services, the sun was brightly shining directly over me. I dreamed that I was in an airplane over the skyline of New York City and was being challenged to step off it and walk on air. I was afraid because there was nothing to hold onto to keep me up if I were to step off the plane, but then when I looked inside the plane for solid things to sustain me, I realized they were not trustworthy because they, too, depend on faith to be held together. So I decided, since I need faith either way, I might as well go ahead and take the challenge. When I did, I did walk on air for a brief moment, and all around me there was an amazing brightness, brighter than the noonday sun.

I woke up and realized that the noonday sun was indeed shining in all its brightness directly over me, but it was very dull in comparison to the glory I'd just seen in the dream. Again, my walk of faith was affirmed.

In 1984, I became associated with Prophetess Dr. Loretta Taylor, of Brooklyn, New York, and learned from her many of the profounder dynamics of prophetic ministry and intercession. Her ministry was of the "Old School" preaching, prayer, and prophecy type. I had already learned by myself how to sit and wait before the Lord in private, but under her ministry I learned to do it in a collective group.

The "Secrets of Prayer and Power" conferences with Billye Brim, of Tulsa, Oklahoma, from 1983 to 1984, also proved a significant part of my spiritual education and empowerment. And, of course, Kenneth E. Hagin's and Kenneth Copeland's conferences and books and tapes have also been life transforming for me, for nearly three decades. There was evidence of God Himself calling and teaching me, but for the grander plan, He has directed me with these and other ministries.

By the time the world-impacting revivals known as the *Toronto Blessing* and the *Pensacola Outpouring* came about, in the mid-1990's, I had already experienced and written extensively on the topics of supernatural experiences and the prophetic.

I was a street preacher (and a subway preacher) for about seven or eight years, and enjoyed countless blessings as I saw God transform lives. One of the greatest street preachers in my neighborhood, the well-known Rev. Luis Zambrano of Graham Avenue in Brooklyn (originally from Ecuador), told me he once asked God to make him like that dynamo preaching over there (me), before he was even saved. Not only did he get gloriously saved, but he became much more successful in street ministry than me, establishing crews with vans and electronic equipment, networking with churches, ministering internationally, and performing miracles of healing more than I ever did. His ministry has lasted over two decades.

During a 70-day prayer time before the Lord in 1986, during which I didn't leave my apartment, I received new direction from the Holy Spirit to teach, preach, prophesy, see visions, and to begin a media ministry that included small booklets, tapes, and drawings. The idea had come to me to cover my windows with cardboard to make the room completely dark so that any lights I see would have to be supernatural. (I learned, however, that the eyes have dynamic activities that produce lights, too; not everything is supernatural.) Using earplugs also became helpful in reducing natural sounds, and in hearing and distinguishing more easily the spiritual ones.

After a couple of years, I removed the cardboard from my windows, and stopped using earplugs. I have found that the Lord still communicates unobstructed. Even if I fall asleep with the television on, any dream or vision

He would produce comes across clearly.

God affirmed and blessed me in my writing and book publishing endeavors, which began in early 1988 with my *Dreams* book, but I could never really get that part of my ministry off the ground. In the meanwhile, I'd begun having dreams instructing me to learn about computers. With all my exposure to the Christian community that believed in the dynamics of the Holy Spirit and revival as I did, I could not find entrance into the "party" that God was throwing and make a transition into a viable ministry in the traditional sense. Traditional ministry models did not accommodate whatever David A. Castro Ministries had to offer; in fact, they challenged that in some cases, as they felt challenged by that. The heavens were open to me with regard to spiritual blessings, but in the natural, every door seemed closed.

But the things of God cannot be boxed in by man-made parameters. The ministry of prophetic revelation is not always the exotic, fashionable, fun thing it often comes across as, and is not supposed to be predictable. Further, we are not supposed to discard fellow believers simply because of their affiliations. The late Kenneth E. Hagin was one of the greatest prophets and Bible teachers of our generation, whom God used in extraordinary signs and wonders and miraculous healing by the Holy Spirit, manifestations often found among Pentecostal believers. Yet, many Pentecostals and their leaders attribute his spiritual manifestations to the work of the devil. How is this possible? Politics in religious circles, resulting in divided flocks disdainful of each other.

Well, what does one do? I, for one, refuse to have unedifying talk with the undiscerning and the unfair. Jesus, thankfully, has instead led me to go to school and brought the festive joy of His party into that journey, transforming and evolving me in the process and, I have come to discover, establishing new ministry models and spaces. With the introduction of new media technologies and communities, truly democratic media production spaces have become a reality. By His grace and divine enabling, I have learned to become autonomous, completely equipped to create anything I want with His passion and permission. The sky is the limit! From age to age and season to season, God does new things and creates new spaces—open doors—for them.

I find it indescribably exciting that God would lead His people into the entertainment industry. Now that His fuller will is becoming clearer to me, I remember that I have often wished I could be an actor and otherwise involved in secular entertainment. Many times, as a little boy, I asked Mom to send me to Hollywood so I could be in movies, or at least send me to acting school. She always said that we can't afford anything like that now, but "Maybe when you grow up, if you're good." Well, I've been good, and I'm all grown up!

It was hard to see that God would allow such a thing during the time that I was trying to become a religious writer and, possibly, a televangelist. (I could have been the next Creflo A. Dollar, in emulation of the great Kenneth Copeland. I could have been a contender!) But with the new, liberating move of the Holy Spirit of God on earth, and the consequent collapse of hegemonic religious structures—both real and imagined—I absolutely see it, believe it, and run to it in full faith knowing that it is not only alright, but it has been a part of God's plan for me from the beginning.

Jeremiah 1:5 Before I formed thee in the belly I knew thee.

Also a colorful development is my newfound less-than-religious view of people and things in life, and my approach to production projects. My re-introduction to the real world, where real people live and move and have their being, which started with attending Drake Business School and The Katharine Gibbs School, included making friends with talented performers. I've met singers, dancers, models, actors—and aspiring ones—and we got along well, occasionally collaborating on school projects. I have maintained close friendships with some (an impressive number of whom are highly spiritual), and they support my dreams to write, produce, direct, and act, and to do it any way I want to do it and to do it til I'm satisfied.

Having studied media production, I feel I have the skills and passion to proceed with confidence, letting the Lord bless me and use me in fresh, colorful and entertaining ways.

Chapter 5: HOW GOD SPEAKS IN VISIONS

There are a number of things that we can do to prepare the way of the Lord in our hearts and lives so that His revelations will be clearer to us. Praying, fasting, asking for the gifts of the Spirit, and studying about these things is always in order. But in the current move of God, in which things have been changed and opened up, it's easier than ever to yield to the Lord, experience His presence, and see visions inspired of Him.

The blockbuster movie *Independence Day* of 1996, starring Will Smith and Jeff Goldblum, has a scene in it with a timely message for us. A scientist says that one of the alien aircraft, which they have had in storage for several decades, and that has a lot of high technology gadgets that they have not seen functioning, has begun to demonstrate its functions in unprecedented ways since its gigantic mother ship began hovering over the earth. Spiritually, we can say that since God's new gigantic anointing has come down to cover the earth, we, His people, are coming alive and demonstrating our functions in unprecedented ways. Papa is coming to get us, and His presence among us is causing a great buzz. New gifts of the Spirit, new boldness and excitement, strength and zest for life, and new ability to see in the realm of the Spirit, are all accessible in measures unprecedented.

The disciples in the Upper Room on the Day of Pentecost (in Acts 2:1-4) yielded fully to the supernatural visitation from on high. They yielded to the supernatural sound of the Holy Ghost visitation as a rushing mighty wind, and because they did yield, the Spirit was able to impart the fuller measure He had come intending. The disciples saw the cloven tongues of fire sitting on each other's heads, and went right ahead and started speaking with other tongues. They didn't decline the visitation but received the whole of it, even though they really didn't know just exactly how He was going to show up.

We have got to have that kind of faith, and not try understanding every little thing. We have been spoiled by too many books and tapes that attempt to dissect everything. Our need to grasp it all before we "get it" has gotten in the way of our getting it. After having studied and learned, and gotten some measure of understanding, we have to finally take the plunge like the early Church fathers did. (I read about three books about the baptism of the Holy Spirit before getting it—not ten.)

Habakkuk 2:1-3 I will stand upon my watch, and set me upon the tower, and will watch to see what He will say unto me, and what I shall answer when I am reproved. And the Lord answered me.

We can stand upon our watch (the post appointed us from the Lord) by faith, just like Habakkuk did. He waited upon the Lord watching to see what the Lord might show him. By an act of his volition, he had said, "I will watch, to see." His faith and act prepared the way for the Lord to talk to him, and He did.

Today also, believers can watch to see what, if anything, the Lord might be pleased to show us. If He will show us things, we will need to be inclined by faith, yielded to the Holy Spirit and pliable in His presence. We cannot get very far in these things if we think something evil will be given us instead. Our heavenly Father will not give us something bad if we ask Him for something good, (Luke 11:9-13).

I have yielded to the Lord countless times and have found Him, and not the devil. When I have seen demonic activity, it wasn't given of the Father; I didn't get deceived because, like Jesus said, "My sheep hear *My* voice, and the voice of another they will not follow," (John 10:4-5). To decline the invitation to come up higher simply because of fear of deception will make the Christian walk dull and lifeless, hence unproductive ultimately. Yielding to the voice of the Lord will enable the transforming power of the Gospel to make us come alive and be interesting, productive, multi-linear, and fun; it will help us to be all that we can be.

Now here is an interesting experience I had when yielding to the Lord. In a dream, Jesus was telling me about a young man that I would soon meet. The Lord told me he would need special attention and education from God's servants because he is a sovereign vessel chosen of God for a special ministry. He also indicated that I would become one of his mentors. As He spoke this to me, I could see the back of this young man's head as he was walking away from me, and it seemed this vision was about to end.

Of my own volition, I decided to speak to the Lord and ask Him if I could see what the young man's face looked like so that I would recognize him when he showed up in my life. I could trust that the Lord would let me know who he is at another time, in some other way, perhaps at the time I would meet him. But out of my present interest and desire to be ready for his appearing—and from impatience—I asked to see his face now.

Still in this vision, I focused my eyes on the back of his head, while praying, "Please turn him around, Jesus, so I can see what he looks like. Please, Lord, turn him around." After a moment or two, the young man turned around and started walking toward me, and I saw his face very clearly. Then I said, "Thank You, Jesus," and then I woke up with full remembrance and understanding of the vision. In time, it actually happened.

This is a clear example of how God may welcome the cooperation of our faith and will in supernatural experiences. If we are willing to communicate with God in the realm of the spirit, ever careful to observe the borders which He would allow us, we may find the Lord hearing and answering our prayer, and communicating with us right there in that realm.

The late William Branham was a twentieth century prophet who saw many astounding visions inspired of the Lord. He explained that many times it seemed as though his inward man would lift himself up and look over a wall to see what was on the other side with his spiritual eyes. In this way, he often saw into the realm of the spirit and received insights about people and situations which the Lord wanted him to respond to with the prayer of faith. This, too, is a clear example of how our own faith and will can cooperate with the Spirit of God in supernatural experiences.

Noteworthy here is the fact that Brother Branham would pierce his eyes into the spiritual realm that way when God was indeed disclosing visions. He was anointed to see, but it was the anointing of the Holy Spirit that permitted him to see. The Prophet Habakkuk stood upon his *watch,* and set himself upon the *tower* because, being in the prophetic/revelatory ministry, he was anointed of God to watch and to see in the realm of the spirit, and he was appointed to a watchtower. When he watched to see *by faith,* the Lord was pleased to disclose some things unto him because of his pure motive—to pray, (Habakkuk 1:1-4).

Having said that, let us also consider the other side of the matter, that in which the Lord may instruct us to not come up. There will be times when the Holy Spirit impresses us not to "break through unto the Lord to gaze" (not to press our eyes in to see a vision at a certain time) lest He *break forth upon us* in some way. When the Israelites approached Mount Sinai at the time God was giving them the Ten Commandments, He clearly warned them "not to *break through to come up unto the Lord,"* otherwise many of them would perish, (Exodus 19:21). And when the Bethshemites *looked into* the Ark of the Lord (which was forbidden them to do), God's anger was kindled and He destroyed over fifty thousand of His own people, (1Samuel 6:19). So He can be grieved in this area, even by His own people today.

In an extremely anointed service, one launched out and prophesied erroneously to an Apostle and his family. Soon afterward, there was a death in his family. It was suggested that the individual was not covered in the prophetic space that he entered, at least not on that occasion. If this is true, it gives us a glimpse of the Holy Spirit dynamic that is not always fun. Then there is the fact of God's respect for others' privacy, and His disinclination to embarrass others. We are not enabled to see so that we can attack and destroy, but to edify, love, empathize, show mercy, and pray. If our motives prove otherwise, we can incur the wrath of God instead of supernatural gifts of God. So, yes, we need to approach these high things in a sober attitude.

If we would approach Him one step at a time, we will be able to discern where to draw the line and not pierce our eyes further. We have got to know how to stay within the borders that the Lord would allow us. This is why it is so important to really know our Lord Jesus, His ways and His moods, and how to cooperate with them.

I always ask the Lord what He's up to when He visits me in any kind of vision. In out-of-body experiences I always try and cooperate with Him, not going where He's not going, and going where He is going. Having grieved Him a few times over the years, I have learned to not test Him or challenge Him in that context. We may, however, talk about it further after we get back home.

THE POWER OF REVELATIONS

2Corinthians 12:1b I will come to... revelations of the Lord.

The great Apostle Paul received many revelations from the Lord. In the context of 2Corinthians 12, after declaring that he will come to visions and revelations of the Lord, he testifies of a particular supernatural experience in which he received both. Throughout the Bible, most visions, both small and great ones, contained some sort of revelation. However, most revelations do not come through visions—they come through simple knowings in the mind or spirit. Paul could also have said, "I will come to study and revelations of the Lord," and, "I will come to prayer and revelations of the Lord."

The word "revelation," (Greek: *apokalupsis*) simply means "an uncovering, an unveiling, a disclosing." The fact that Paul uses this word alongside "visions," shows us that they are closely related and that, as in his own experience, visions can provide revelations of the mysteries of the Gospel.

When a revelation does come in a supernatural way, it is either because God wants to teach us something new in such a way that we won't miss or forget it, or because He just happens to be speaking that way in that season of time, or because we would not believe or receive it any other way. In Paul's case, it seems God spoke to him through an abundance of supernatural revelations for all of these reasons.

God is always giving revelations. We are to go from revelation to revelation, always building upon the foundation of the Word of God, "Till we all come in the unity of the faith, and of the knowledge of the Son of God, unto a perfect man, unto the measure of the stature of the fullness of Christ," (Ephesians 4:13).

Obviously, this does not mean that "we are to go from vision to vision or from trance to trance or from heavenly visitation to heavenly visitation. We are to receive God's regular disclosings as we study His Word, pray, and serve Him by faith. But as we do so, we may occasionally receive some disclosings of His Spirit in supernatural ways. Supernatural revelations support, confirm, and otherwise strengthen that which we have been receiving from God's Word by faith; they give us new spiritual ground upon which we have not yet tread; and they may also correct us from some error that we may have been walking in.

Ephesians 1:17-18a That the God of our Lord Jesus Christ, the Father of glory, may give unto you the spirit of wisdom and revelation in the knowledge of Him: The eyes of your understanding being enlightened.

By having the spirit of wisdom and revelation in the knowledge of Christ, the eyes of our understanding may be enlightened so that we may see what God may reveal to us, howsoever He may be pleased to do so. Our salvation (Greek: *soteria* = "deliverance in every area") depends on our coming unto the knowledge of the truth, (1Timothy 2:4). "Through knowledge will the righteous be delivered," (Proverbs 11:9b). Yet, there are many people who study knowledge and still are never able to come to the knowledge of the truth (2Timothy 3:7) and, therefore, they never receive their full deliverance. This is because they do not have the *spirit* of knowledge, the *spirit* of wisdom, and the *spirit* of revelation.

The grace of God that brings salvation has appeared to all men (Titus 2:11), but not all men receive the love of the truth so that they might be saved, (2Thessalonians 2:10). Therefore, they do not receive the spirit of revelation for the acknowledging of Christ which the God of our Lord Jesus Christ is freely giving.

Without the spirit of wisdom and revelation in the knowledge of Him, we will not be able to hear the hidden wisdom being spoken by the Holy Spirit. God reveals things unto our spirits by His Spirit, so a person without the Holy Spirit does not have ears to hear what the Spirit speaks. If he walks in the things of God (if he goes to Church, reads the Bible, or prays) it is only in the flesh, as he has been taught by tradition. He has not been born-again, and is not truly alive unto God in the spirit. So what does he need? A supernatural revelation from the Holy Spirit which shows him his need to be born-again.

A revelation is a sort of unfolding of a message or insight from the Lord. A message may involve the past, present, or future, and an insight may involve some light on God's Word or character, or a person, or a situation. A message or insight can be revealed in a great variety of ways. God speaks in many different ways.

Frequently, when God gave a revelation in the Bible, He used natural things to teach us spiritual truths. This shows us that His creation issued from Him, behaves naturally as its Creator, and, therefore, speaks clearly and constantly of Him. Therefore, we are without excuse. All of us, in some way or other, have heard from God, (Romans 1:20).

Greek philosophers (as those of Paul's time) also learned some things about God from the natural things around them, (Acts 17:28). Only when they tried to get spiritual revelations to learn about Him did they get into trouble because they had no foundation in that arena.

That God reveals something to us is extremely important, and can be very powerful as well. A supernatural revelation from the Lord can provide the key that will open heavenly portals, (and open doors in the earth, too). Such a revelation can also become the basis for our life, our ministry, our future, our kind of faith, and our kind of walk with Him. It is for having received a revelation from God that Paul's life (and, consequently, world history) was dramatically transformed.

Although the revelation of Jesus to Paul while he was on the road to Damascus (Acts 9:3-6) was a sovereign move of God which did not depend on his faith and yieldedness, Paul obviously embraced the revelation. Thereafter he had faith to yield to further visions and revelations of the Lord, even an abundance of them.

When it was revealed to Peter that Jesus was the Christ, the Anointed One from God, he was able to exclaim it boldly and emphatically. As a result, Jesus then gave him the keys of the Kingdom of Heaven, which involved awesome supernatural powers, (Matthew 16:13-19).

Revelations do not have to come in supernatural ways in order to be real and valid. Indeed, most revelations are disclosed to the spirit and the mind—via simple insights—and enable us to walk by faith in that which has been revealed. God speaks in many ways which are not so spectacular and supernatural. And when we obey even the simplest of His leadings and revelations, we will be walking in the spirit where God Himself is.

John 20:29 Blessed are they that have not seen, and yet have believed.

There are many kinds of supernatural manifestations that the Lord may operate. An important aspect of His workings involves our cooperation, and that requires faith. It is, therefore, important that we learn to listen and watch for His revelations unto us (in visions, dreams, impressions, and other ways in which He speaks) because faith comes by hearing and hearing by the "Word" (Greek: *rhema* = "current revelation or message") of God, (Romans 1 0:17).

Even though God is sovereign, and will often work His signs and wonders independently of our faith, knowledge, understanding, and will, He often will not. He is often limited by our limitations. He is often able to do only as much as we can believe Him for. And He is always looking for people who believe Him to be able to do anything, and with whose cooperation He can operate. Remember, we are called to be laborers together with God, (1Corinthians 3:9).

The gifts of the Spirit are an excellent example of this. They show the manifestation of the Holy Spirit, as He wills, but will not operate without our cooperation and input because they are *given unto us,* (1Corinthians 12:8-10). Other supernatural manifestations (such as angelic visitations, walking on water, fire in the sky, appearances of the Shekinah Glory Cloud, and others) are not given to us in the same sense as are the nine spiritual gifts. Yet an understanding about these greater manifestations, or a lack of it, can also determine whether or not they will occur among a people.

This is one reason why God instructed me to write about signs and wonders. He told me to study about all kinds of supernatural experiences of the Lord, and to teach about them, because He is getting ready to pour out His Spirit in the greatest revival this world has ever seen. He said that the supernatural will be a major part of this revival, including visions and dreams.

Acts 2:17 (amp) And it shall come to pass in the last days, God declares, that I will pour out of my Spirit upon all mankind, and your sons and your daughters shall prophesy—telling forth the divine counsels—and your young men shall see visions (that is, divinely granted appearances), and your old men shall dream [divinely suggested] dreams.

As I sat at my desk studying one day, in the summer of 1988, I became so excited about what I was learning, and about what God was getting ready to do, that my spirit leaped up and asked Him "God! What are You gonna do!?" And He answered, "I'm gonna do *something!*" Wow! He answered me! He's gonna do *"something!"* A few days later, I dreamed that I was excitedly telling a friend of mine (who was laying down and relaxing on a bed), "God *is doing* something!"

Reader, there is a revelation from God for us here. The Body of Christ (symbolized by my friend in the dream) is largely idle and relaxing in comfort (the bed). And the Lord is sending excited messengers to awaken and alert the Church to the fact that God is getting ready to do something great and supernatural. He is bringing some great supernatural demonstrations of His Spirit to magnify His Name. And so that we will be able to apprehend and work together with Him in the great revival that is virtually upon us, He would impart unto us a practical understanding of supernatural experiences.

The supernatural can be taught. Revelations that are inspired of the Lord can precede, incite, and be the key to supernatural experiences. Where there is no "revelation" (Hebrew: *chazown* = "mental sight, dream, revelation, oracle, vision"), the people perish, (Proverbs 29:18a). Where there are revelations, the people have the power to prosper.

May the *spirit of revelation* come upon the pure and willing hearts, that by it, great and mighty things which we, as yet, know not, will not be strange to us at the time of their manifestation. As John at Patmos Island, may we, wherever we are, hear the voice of the Good Shepherd, see the doors of heaven open, and enjoy discourse from there.

Revelation 4:1 After this I looked, and behold, a door was opened in Heaven: and the first voice which I heard was as it were of a trumpet talking with me; which said, Come up hither, and I will show thee things which must be hereafter.

The Apostle John at this point is over eighty years of age. He has known Jesus since his youth, (he was the youngest of Jesus' main twelve disciples). He knew Jesus in the flesh and in the spirit, and received the Word of God directly from the Master.

Now imprisoned for preaching, he has plenty of time to review in his spirit and mind all he's gained hitherto of the teachings, revelations, and prophecies of the Lord. I observe that perhaps he sought to understand the end of those things which Jesus began both to do and teach, for the end of all things was not yet written. They were now to be written (in the Book of Revelation) partly to answer John's questions which he evidently inquired of the Lord during this time of imprisonment wherein he could meditate deeply without interruption.

John knew the Lord Jesus as the beginning, Alpha, but not as the end, Omega. When on the Lord's day Jesus speaks to him, He first says something with which he can "bear witness" in his spirit, "I Am Alpha," then He takes him further, "and Omega", the First and the Last, the Beginning and the Ending. (Revelation 1:11.)

Jesus commenced, in Revelation chapters two and three, to speak to John of the churches that existed then, their present state, and the mind of God concerning them. These brought great confirmation and illumination to John, therefore he was able to receive well Jesus' greater message, namely that of the future, in His "Come up here, and I will show you things which must be hereafter," (Rev. 4:1).

When Jesus is taking us in a supernatural experience to receive a greater revelation of Him than we already have, He will meet us first where we're at, where we can bear witness with Him, then He leads us into a more perfect understanding.

Cornelius, an Italian man, was a devout proselyte to the Jewish religion. In Acts 10:1-6, when the Angel of God visited him, he didn't tell him, "Your religion is wrong, you've got to repent of your sins and come to Jesus and receive the Holy Ghost and pray in tongues!" The Angel didn't even mention the Jewish tradition. He met Cornelius where he would receive him, "Your prayers and good deeds are acceptable to God," (Acts 10:4).

With these words with which Cornelius bore witness, for they were a true testimony of him, the Angel could take him further to the next step of a "new revelation" of the God he already served. This way Cornelius was able to receive the instruction to hear Peter's words about the new birth and the baptism in the Holy Ghost with power, (verses 5-8).

Similarly, though not in a supernatural way, Apollos was able to receive of

Aquila and Priscilla revelations of "The Way" more perfectly, (Acts 18:24-28).

Acts 18:24-28 This man was instructed in the way of the Lord; and being fervent in the spirit, he spake and taught diligently the things of the Lord, knowing only the baptism of John. And he began to speak boldly in the synagogue: whom when Aquila and Priscilla had heard, they took him unto them, and expounded unto him the way of God more perfectly.

Apollos always kept up-to-date with what God was doing. Though born in Egypt, he highly esteemed the tradition of the fathers and obeyed the Law of Moses. He was mighty in the Scriptures, and zealous, so he was able to receive John the Baptist's revelation "Prepare ye the way of the Lord." He was also faithful and diligent to preach as much as was in him. When a new revelation came concerning the same Way, yet more perfectly, he embraced it because it was founded on the Word he'd already received.

Aquila and Priscilla met him first where he was at in the Word. They agreed with him about the Law of Moses, then about the Ministry of John the Baptist. Now that they met, and understood, and validated where he was coming from, he was open to receive a more perfect understanding of "The Way." Doubtless he'd already heard of Jesus of Nazareth but wasn't instructed in detail of Him up to that time. But the Holy Ghost used this time to prompt a hunger and thirst for the truth of Him, so that at the fullness of the time Jesus the Christ might come and quench the thirsting of his soul.

The Body of Christ is now thirsting for Heaven, that more perfect City. We've been so gradually more and more for nearly two thousand years. Jesus is about to quench our thirst—first, little by little, finally, with a shout, the voice of the Arch-angel, the trump of God!

When Jesus says, "Come up hither", He first comes to us where we're at and are able to receive Him, and He offers His hand in a way we can receive it.

We're supposed to have faith and put our hand in His and say, "Yes, Jesus, I will go where You take me, Good Shepherd. Yea, though I walk through a new path unknown to me, a new revelation, a more perfect understanding, I will not fear for You are with me. Your Word Comforts, and enlightens me—keeps me in sound doctrine and unadulterated revelation so that I will not be confused or deceived. Yes, Lord, here am I, send me into that higher height and deeper depth of Your Word by the revelation of the Holy Ghost. Yes, Lord, I incline to visions and revelations of Thee." Be they supernatural visions and revelations or be they greater knowledge and understanding of God's written Word, we are to be open to the Spirit of God and to the growth He desires for us.

Portals, entrances, openings are coming in the air wherein he that hath an eye to see may see visions of the Lord. The supernatural realm allows, seeks, violent faith; the violent, bold, daring, fearless, take it by force, (Matthew 11:12). We take it by force—enter into the spiritual realm—not by causing supernatural experiences ourselves, but by believing God's Word with regard to this area and yielding to His visitations howsoever they may come. And if He wills, He may show us some things in the spirit and we'll be yielded. The Holy Spirit truly is willing; we who are flesh are weak in this area.

But thank God faith, great faith, faith in all areas, comes, and comes more, and comes more and more, by hearing, and hearing more, and hearing, reading, and receiving more and more of the Word of God, (Romans 10:17).

Let's be willing to become familiar with experiences that are in the celestial plane—our citizenship, our inheritance, is in that dimension. When Jesus calls us up There in the Rapture of the Glorious Church, the Body of Christ as a whole shouldn't find completely foreign to us what we'll then see.

The latter-day explosive visitation of angels is so that we can be served by invisible beings to fulfill the Great Commission in the visible world, and then be taken into the invisible. As we draw nearer to the latter it will become more visible to us, and the former more invisible. He that has ears to hear, let him hear what the Spirit is saying unto the Church, (Revelation 3:22).

The Spirit of Knowledge and Understanding

Colossians 1:9-10 For this cause we also, since the day we heard it, do not cease to pray for you, and to desire that you might be filled with the knowledge of His will in all wisdom and spiritual understanding: That you might walk worthy of the Lord unto all pleasing, being fruitful in every good work, and increasing in the knowledge of God.

The Apostle Paul prays here by the Holy Ghost that the Christians of Colosse, and also all Christians, would be filled with the knowledge of God's will. This means we've got to read the whole Bible, over and over again. All wisdom and spiritual understanding come from God's Word. And since His Word is alive it'll prosper in us and make us fruitful in every area of our lives. His Word is eternal, so it'll forever continue to increase our knowledge of God.

Much knowledge has been handed down in the Body of Christ, spiritual and doctrinal. From generation to generation since God's Word has been in the earth, God's people have been growing gradually more and more. We are not to take lightly the knowledge available through the insights, experiences, and personal encounters with God gained by those who have come and gone before us.

The two-thousand-year-old Church now needs just a few more finishing touches to be glorious, to be made ready for the coming of the Bridegroom, which is near at hand. We're seeing glimpses of what will be during the Millennial Reign of Christ.

The Word of God has multiplied, and is multiplying still. That which has been planned for the pre-Millennial Church is alive in the earth now for those who believe and walk in the Spirit.

Now some are ever learning and never coming to the knowledge of the truth. This is because they lean onto their own understanding as they gain knowledge. We must lean onto the Holy Spirit as we gain knowledge and He will give us a living understanding. Our own understanding, our carnal mind, cannot please God.

Romans 8:5-8 For they that are after the flesh do mind the things of the flesh; but they that are after the Spirit the things of the Spirit. For to be carnally minded is death; but to be spiritually minded is life and peace. Because the carnal mind is enmity against God: for it is not subject to the law of God, neither indeed can be. So then they that are in the flesh cannot please God.

But with faith it is possible to please Him, (Hebrews 11:6). By faith we believe that God has given us an understanding, a quick understanding, (Isaiah 11:3). This is also known as the mind of Christ, so that we may search and know all things, yes, the deep things of God. For the Spirit searches all things as a springing, running river of living water.

So as we read God's Word continually we will have not a stagnant, carnal form of knowledge and understanding which is unteachable, unpliable, and unable to receive fresh manna. But allowing the living Spirit to quicken, make alive our understanding we can increase and run from glory to glory to glory, by the Spirit of the Lord, (1Corinthians 2; 2Corinthians 3:17-18).

The Heavens are Open

The Word of God is being multiplied in the current season, and therefore, prophecies are increasing, and visions and dreams are increasing.

Acts 2:17-19 And it shall come to pass in the last days, saith God, I will pour out of My Spirit upon all flesh: and your sons and your daughters shall prophesy, and your young men shall see visions, and your old men shall dream dreams: And on my servants and on my handmaidens I will pour out in those days of My Spirit; and they shall prophesy: And I will show wonders in heaven above, and signs in the earth beneath; blood, and fire, and vapor of smoke.

The Blood of Jesus first washes our sins away when we become believers. Then the fire of the Holy Ghost baptizes and sanctifies our bodies which are His Temple. Then the vapor of smoke, the glory of the Lord, fills His temple, as the Spirit of the Lord is poured upon and out of us. We're the spout where the glory pours out! That's why we must become fit for the Master's use, prepared unto every good work, (2Timothy 2:21).

Smoke rises, so as God pours out His Spirit unto us, and we release it back unto Him, we're giving Him glory, and a connection is made between earth (our earthly tabernacle, this physical body) and heaven (the true tabernacle, which the Lord pitched). This connection between heaven and earth is the result of man being reconciled unto God by faith in the Blood sacrifice of Jesus Christ on the Cross of Calvary. This living relationship opens the heavens unto us so that we may receive blessings, directions, and literal insights from our Father who is in the Third Heaven.

Ezekiel 1:1b The heavens were opened, and I saw visions of God.

He is the same yesterday, today, and forever, (Hebrews 13:8); there isn't even a shadow of changing with Him, (James 1:17). Therefore this experience of Ezekiel is current for us today. The heavens are being disclosed and the Body of Christ is observing visions and revelations of the Lord as never before. No wonder the world also is finding great interest in these areas, albeit not according to truth.

As Ezekiel was taken up often by the Spirit of the Lord, so shall the Body of Christ also become more accustomed than we have been to "rapture drills" before the "main event." Let's have faith and no fear to incline to these as did Ezekiel, Paul, John, and others chronicled in the Written Word of God.

KINDS OF VISIONS AND DREAMS

1: Spiritual Vision

This is like an "invisible vision." Inwardly you know you are seeing something in your spirit, but it's not clear enough to be able to describe in terms of pictures. This is usually the first type of vision which the Holy Spirit uses to get our attention so He can show us more. Yielding to this first *wooing* of the Lord can result in a greater vision of Him.

When Jesus was on earth, He walked in the spirit and was always led by the Holy Spirit, and He talked with God. However, He did not constantly see spectacular [pictorial] visions. Where the Bible says that He spoke that which He had *seen* with the Father (John 8:38), it can mean both a supernatural [visible] sight and an inspired [invisible] impression that He felt coming from the heart of the Father. What Jesus had seen from Him, (from the Greek word *hŏraō* = "perceive, discern, or attend to, physically *or* mentally"), does not invariably mean that He literally saw describable visions each time God wanted to speak with Him.

When Jesus *saw* (from the Greek word *ĕidō* = "understand, be sure, be aware, or see, literally *or* figuratively") Nathaniel and *knew* that he was an honest person (John 1:47-48), that *knowing* also came from a divinely inspired assurance that may or may not have involved a distinct [visible] vision. So there are gray areas—and not always clear-cut distinctions—between the different kinds of visions.

Jesus had to walk by faith just as we do if He was going to show us how to follow the leadings of the Holy Spirit by faith. Without faith it is impossible to please God (Hebrews 11:6), therefore, we can understand that Jesus, in His human form, had to test the spirits whether they were of God just as we do. He pleased God by faith by trying to understand and interpret the thoughts, promptings, impressions, hunches, and gut-feelings which He experienced *invisibly*—that is, by not-so-visible *spiritual* visions.

Now every Christian has a measure of *spiritual eyesight* because the Lord is in each one helping us to discern His will for our lives, But a *spiritual vision* specifically occurs when a significant view catches the spiritual eye, a view which one can begin to describe as a revelation from the Lord even though it has no distinct image and cannot be described pictorially as our second type of vision can be.

When we are praying for someone or prophesying to them we often say, "I don't know what it is, but I'm getting a sense of..." or "I seem to be almost seeing...," or "I'm vaguely perceiving..." Such vague descriptions may indicate that the person so ministering is seeing with the spiritual eyes. The appropriate response is to translate into one's own understanding and words the message he believes the Lord is revealing. When the person is led by the Holy Spirit, and his understanding is biblically-based, the prayer or prophecy will prove to be a blessing to the hearer.

2: Pictorial Vision

This one is a step up from the *spiritual vision.* Here, an image does indeed begin to show up in the mind of the one who sees it, and he can begin to describe it in terms of pictures.

The most common and least spectacular type of *pictorial vision* is one in which no special tangible anointing is in manifestation. The person who receives it is not entranced, over-powered, or otherwise overwhelmed by the presence of God, and no profound symbolic features are involved. It would, instead, be characterized by a sort of simplified picture, symbolic or not, which appears for a very short moment, in a flash, with no motion, as a photograph.

A more spectacular manifestation of this type of vision may occur when one is in the spirit, under a special anointing of the Holy Spirit, and he begins to see such pictures, perhaps one right after another, as if being shown some photographs. And each of these "photographs" may or may not be related. This type of revealing to the mind occurs rather instantly, as, for example, when a minister declares from the platform, "The Lord is giving me a revelation (such as a manifestation of a *word of knowledge,* or a *word of wisdom;* or the *discerning of spirits;* 1Corinthians 12:8,10), that someone in the congregation has a [particular] condition, and He wants to heal you right now." Then the minister proceeds to share another such "word" with the congregation, one which is unrelated and also instant in coming and leaving. It is in our next type of vision (a *panoramic vision)* that such an image lingers for a moment or two with intent to show motion or progression of some kind.

These kinds of visions, for the most part, can occur with our eyes open or closed. And this is true of most visions. It really doesn't matter except for the fact that natural sights can distract us from spiritual sights, so it can be helpful to close our eyes when we are yielding to the Holy Spirit to see visions.

3: <u>Panoramic Vision</u>

Here, a series of events is "unrolled" before one's eyes, again in terms of pictures, with or without symbolism, and can last a few moments. Such as when Saul of Tarsus (who later is called Paul) saw a vision of Ananias coming into his room and then praying for him to be healed (Acts 9:12), as our cover design depicts. (I'm 19 in the photograph used in Paul's role.)

This type of vision can best be described as a *pictorial vision in motion.* It has all the same characteristics except that it is more like a strip of video film instead of just one exposure of one frame, as in photographic film which shows only still pictures. Webster's Dictionary defines "panorama" as "a picture unrolled before the spectator in such a way as to give the impression of a continuous view."

When my mother was a little girl, her father was the Pastor of a small Church. She has told me that it would often occur during testimony time that people would go up to the front and declare that they had seen "a vision from the Lord." Often such visions came "in the night." Most dreams are *panoramic night visions.* When we are asleep, we are less distracted from such "movies" and, therefore, God uses the opportunity to show us more, (Job 33:14-16).

In one such testimony during testimony time, a certain lady got up and said she had just had a dream that morning that the airplane which my grandfather (who was a pioneering Pentecostal Pastor) was scheduled to be on later that week would crash. So she warned him to reschedule his missionary trip to Puerto Rico. Well, he did. And the airplane did crash. And, though there was mourning for the victims of that tragedy, there was gladness that my grandfather's life was saved. Salvation in any form can result from any form of vision from the Lord when we take heed to it.

4: Dream (Night Vision)

A *dream* is "a vision of the night." In a simple dream inspired by the Holy Spirit, anyone or any combination of the three foregoing types of visions can operate, but here the person is asleep. Because he is at rest, his night visions can be lengthier than day ones, and more difficult to remember or to interpret.

This is because dreams have the tendency to occur one right after another, and they also seem to involve more complex symbolism than the other visions.

In Psalms 16:7 & 77:6, the Bible shows us that our own human mind, will, emotions and intellect, are largely involved in the dreaming process. This is so, whether or not we are born-again and led by the Holy Spirit and have the mind of Christ. The mental apparatus that God created in us works in certain ways irrespective of its input and output. We will have dreams whether they are for our spiritual good or not.

Dreams often reflect our lifestyles, our relationship with God, and our diligence to obey His Word (or lack thereof). The thoughts, motives, and intentions of our hearts speak loudly to us in dreams. They seem to be repeated back to us in the night seasons in revised versions—versions that depict a more root-of-the-matter kind of perspective on ourselves. In a sense, we might say that people, subconsciously and involuntarily, preach the truth to themselves via dreams; and we may also say that God, too, preaches the truth to us via dreams.

Dreams are more within our jurisdiction and responsibility to watch over than are other visions. We can ask God to show us other kinds of visions and He may or may not do so. But we know we are going to have dreams even if we don't ask for them, so it behooves us to educate and train our dream processes so as to make them conducive to spiritual revelations that will enhance our lives for good. Will God mind us waking up our dream mechanism by our own volition? The answer is found here: The dream mechanism is going to work anyway, just as our own mind is going to work anyway. So, as God expects us to study to show ourselves approved unto Him in day things, so also in night things. We are the ones who need to apply ourselves to renew our minds to the Word of God so that He can show up in any and every area of our lives. Even when He shows up in supernatural dreams, they will not always operate independently of our learning.

5: Audible Message

By any of a great variety of voices or sounds, the Lord can disclose messages. Such a message can be audible in the literal sense that the physical, external ear can hear it, but usually it is only audible to the spiritual, internal ear. That's why when someone says that God just spoke distinctly to them, others nearby usually didn't hear Him.

The highest and most supernatural kind of *audible message* is that which involves the voice of God the Father, audibly to the external ears. This is very rare now, but it occurred in the Bible several times.

Jesus spoke to Saul (who later is called Paul) when he was on his way to Damascus (Acts 9:3-7), and this was external and audible because the men that were with him also heard the voice of Jesus. This is very rare also, but it can occur.

When we hear Jesus speaking distinctly to us in our hearts, it may be by His own revelation directly to us. But most of the time He sends His Holy Spirit to testify of Him, (John 15:26). Jesus said that the Holy Spirit will receive [messages] of Him and shall show them unto us (John 16:14); the Spirit shall hear Jesus speaking, and then He will speak that unto us, (John 16:13).

Now whereas the voice of Jesus is more clear and discernible, the voice of the Holy Spirit seems to take on many different sounds and forms and tones and moods. He may sound like the voice of a person that you know, or like your own voice; He may even sound like an inanimate object (a car, a door, a machine, a musical instrument). Such are the various kinds of voices, noises, and sounds which the Spirit may use to speak a certain thing unto us, in just such a way that we can get what He's trying to say.

Our own spirit, too, has a variety of ways to speak to us; he knows what's in us, what our makeup is, and how to preach to us in just such a way that we'll get the message. The difficult thing to determine is whether it is our born-again godly spirit that is speaking to us, or our carnal-minded thoughts. This is why we need the Word of God, to help us make a clear distinction between natural (unspiritual) thoughts, hunches, impressions and ideas, and those which are spiritual and for our benefit, (Hebrews 4:12).

6: Apparition

Here a person sees a being that literally appears to him seemingly "out of thin air." The appearance may be seen with the natural eyes open or closed, and it may even be a tangible experience. It may be perceived physically—the being's presence may be felt—without being obviously seen. It is an *appearing,* a *visiting,* but not necessarily a *sighting.*

An *apparition* is different from a *pictorial vision* in that it is an actual—perhaps tangible and audible—visitation occurring outside of the person. Pictorial visions, by themselves, are not actual experiences but only revelations with images shown to the mind by the Holy Spirit. In a pictorial vision, any person, place, or thing (or any combination of these) can be shown to the mind. In an apparition, however, places and objects cannot actually appear to a person, but a person, or an angel, or Jesus can.

In an apparition, those who have died cannot be involved in a literal way. Many people believe that a dead person, such as a loved one who recently died, has appeared to them in this type of vision. But this cannot be so because the Bible strictly forbids communication with the dead, (Deuteronomy 18:9-14). Therefore, the only explanation is this: either the image of the dead person is being produced by some sort of demonic spirit trying to deceive the person seeing it; or the person's subconscious mind is producing that image because it brings comfort to him; or, if it is really a supernatural revelation from God involving the dead person appearing, the part of it involving the dead person can only be a visual symbol at best. God may accommodate the subconscious thought process and allow it to incite subjective symbols because of their particular ability to resonate with us and provoke certain responses. Visual revelations with symbolic representations of people can be found in actual supernatural experiences such as trances, audible voices, and apparitions.

The dead are not really "with us;" they cannot literally leave their eternal abode and plainly appear unto us, but may only be seen symbolically or figuratively, as in a *pictorial vision, dream,* or *trance.* Also in an *audible message*, we will not literally hear the actual voice of someone who has died, but we might hear a symbolic representation of their voice. People who are no longer on earth cannot plainly speak to us in an actual, literal way. Therefore, if we hear their voice in any kind of vision, it can only be a symbolic voice, used by God strictly because of our relational perception of the person represented by that voice. The stuff of symbols (their essential nature) is mostly found in its ability to appeal to human emotions and perceptions.

Why would God give someone a vision that permits a symbol of a person who has died, knowing that he or she may think it was much more than just symbolic? If the person believes that they had an apparition of a dead loved one, wouldn't that make God jealous? Yes, but He is more concerned with the message that can encourage that person in the things of God than He is with the means by which He may have to appeal to his natural emotional disposition at the cognitive level, which may allow images from a vast range of memories. God will not, by some sort of due process, instantly judge us for processing thoughts with the mental apparatus that we're working with. He knows our thoughts and ways are lower than His, but He uses them anyway, even in supernatural revelations.

Rarely does a revelation come with an explanatory teaching that qualifies it, even though it may cause wrong thinking on the part of the one who receives it. Many good people think God permits communication with the dead because

Joan of Arc, a saint who lived long ago, heard audible voices of departed saints which inspired her to do mighty things for God. At the expense of their wrong thinking, God used the best means He saw fit to communicate to Joan because in His usage of symbols, there is a dynamic in which wisdom is justified of her fruit.

If we can understand this, then we won't get so caught up with a vision of a dead loved one, even if it comes in a special way; we will seek to understand the message and not go off on a tangent. And if we do not understand God's usage of that symbolic image, we might start cherishing a feeling of the dead one as if he is "still with us." If we can understand these points, we will be able to detect when the enemy is trying to deceive us, and then we can reject his devices, in the Name of Jesus.

7: Divine Sight

More than just a *spiritual vision* or symbolic representation, a *divine sight* is an actual disclosing of a supernatural event. It is a lot like an *apparition* in that it is an actual occurrence outside of the person or persons experiencing it. But here it is not a being, but an object or activity in the spiritual realm being disclosed to the natural realm.

It was a *divine sight* when the angel of the Lord appeared to Moses in a flame of fire out of the midst of a bush, (Exodus 3:2-5). This great sight which Moses saw, and the great voice he heard, was God in divine manifestation. He conversed with Moses on this holy ground, and commissioned and anointed him to deliver His people Israel from Egyptian bondage.

As the Egyptians pursued the Israelites to destroy them, God's angel came between their two camps to protect His people. This was a corporate *divine sight* because it was visible to everyone involved. That angel had been guiding Israel all throughout their deliverance. He was constantly in their sight as a pillar of cloud by day, and as a pillar of fire by night, (Exodus 13:21-22). But now in the presence of their enemies, this angel of God becomes a cloud of darkness to the Egyptian camp, while remaining a light to Israel.

Other accounts of *divine sights* are: 1) when the Lord descended upon Mount Sinai in the form of thunders and lightnings and fire and smoke, (Exodus 19:16-18); 2) when Moses and the elders of Israel saw God upon Mount Sinai with a paved work of a sapphire stone under His feet, (Exodus 24:9-10); 3) when the Shekinah Glory Cloud of the Lord filled the Temple at its dedication, (2Chronicles 5:13-14); and 4) when a light from the sky, which was disclosed in the first heaven (our immediate atmosphere), shone round about Saul (Paul) on the road to Damascus at the time of his conversion, (Acts 26:13-19). In this latter case, when Paul testified of this supernatural experience he called it "the heavenly vision," and it was accompanied by the *audible voice* of Jesus.

8: Open Heaven

In this type of vision, a hole appears in the immediate sky, the celestial realm is disclosed, and heavenly sights of God become seeable.

The Prophet Ezekiel said, "The heavens were opened, and I saw visions of God," (Ezekiel 1:1-4). In the verses that follow, he goes on to share one of the most detailed visions described in the Bible. He first sees a great cloud, sent by God to protect him from His brightness (as occurred with Moses and the children of Israel at Mount Sinai), and then he sees flashing lightning ("fire infolding itself"), brilliant light, angels, and other details.

Notice how he declares that "the heavens were opened" first, before he began to see the visions of God. In a sense great or small, I think there first comes a sort of opening in the realm of the spirit before any kind of disclosing can occur. And there are many different kinds of disclosings from God which can occur.

A Christian can seem to walk under an *open heaven* in the sense that he has been peculiarly anointed in a certain area of ministry. When he is in the spirit, a special authority in the Holy Ghost may come upon him emboldening him to say and do certain things that he would not ordinarily say or do, and Jesus will say "Amen" to those things and they will have the intended effect.

Evangelist Arthur Blessitt walks under an open heaven in the sense that he can impact nations with the Gospel, some which most other ministers are unable to enter. Apostle Heidi Baker walks under an open heaven in the sense that dramatic healings and miracles occur in her ministry in extraordinary ways. Sometimes an open heaven in someone's life is like a divine favor that facilitates the supernatural almost as if by no effort on their part. God just seems to show up with great ease as they walk in the spirit, and the results can be seen in the natural realm.

An *open heaven* in manifestation as a specific kind of vision is characterized by a sort of veil being lifted, clouds rolling back, the sky being loosened, and distant and dim things being made near and clear. In my experience, this type of vision occurs in a captivating, almost trance-like state, when I'm by myself. Open heaven visions can facilitate revelations of the future more than the simpler kinds of visions because the things of the future are still "in the air"— they have not yet come down to earth—they are still in their formation state. It seems to me, then, that the things to come (future events) which were revealed to the Apostle John when he was on Patmos Island, came to him because a *door in heaven* was opened up for him and summoned him there to see, (Revelation 4:1-2).

9: Trance

In a *trance,* the Holy Spirit comes over a person like a heavy blanket and, in the greater cases, stupefies or paralyzes him temporarily. In such a state, a great many kinds of visions may be imparted. Many people receive visions and revelations of the Lord via trances. Now some trances are not so much vision experiences as they are demonstrations of God's power over the physical body. There are trances without visions which God gives for purposes other than to reveal things.

God said, "I will pour out of My Spirit upon... *flesh,* (Acts 12:17). This word "flesh" is translated from the Greek word *sarx* which means "fleshly meat, carnal, animal, physical body." This means that in the last days God will pour out of His Spirit upon physical bodies in tangible ways, as when Peter *fell* into a trance, (Acts 10:10); when the hand of God *fell* upon Ezekiel, (Ezekiel 8:1); when the priests *fell* to the floor and could not stand up, (2Chronicles 5:14) or walk, (2Chronicles 7:2); when Daniel was in a *deep sleep from the Lord,* (Daniel 10:9); and when Job's bones *shook and trembled* in the visions of the night, (Job 4:14).

10: Out-of-Body Experience

The Word of God teaches us that the human makeup consists in three parts: spirit, soul, and body, (1Thessalonians 5:23). You are a spirit, you have a soul (which is your mind), and you live in a physical body. In natural thoughts and wanderings, your soul can partly travel anywhere you can imagine. Similarly, in spiritual and supernatural revelations, your soul—together with your spirit— can go outside the borders of your normal mental frame and travel in the spiritual dimension by the Spirit of the Lord.

This kind of supernormal experience involves the soul, so it is rightly called "soul travel." It is also known as "astral projection" because one's spirit is somewhat projected forth out of its normal boundaries and enabled to fly freely in celestial places, aiming toward the stars, almost without limit. The person's spirit does not entirely leave the body, although there are degrees of his absence from the body, for the life essence must remain in order to sustain its normal functions, such as the heartbeat and respiration.

People can train themselves to be able to do this by the power of their own will, but they should not. It is only when God initiates an *out-of-body experience* that we may freely yield and give ourselves to it and know that we will be fully protected in the realm of the spirit. Without His initiating such an experience, the special anointing of God's presence, God's armor, and God's angels that we need for safety in that realm are not imparted. Therefore, in such cases, a person places himself in a position of vulnerability to deception and trouble from evil spirits if he practices projecting his own spirit out of his body by acts of his own volition.

The Apostle Paul teaches us one of the most important principles involved in supernatural experiences which are of God (1Corinthians 5:3-5), and it applies to any kind of supernatural experience which is of the Lord. He shows us that it must be "In the Name of our Lord Jesus Christ," and "With the power of our Lord Jesus Christ." That is to say, it must both bring glory to Jesus, and proceed from the power of His anointing—it must both begin and end with our Lord Jesus Christ. It is only then that He is in our supernatural experiences and that they will prove a blessing.

11: Translation

The experience of *supernatural translation* is the literal dematerializing of a person's physical body and his rematerializing in another place. It is also known as *supernatural translocation* and *supernatural transportation*. When this occurs, it is an actual physical experience, and not a vision. But I list it here along with our kinds of visions because it usually begins with and depends on some kind of vision from the Lord. Visions, voices, angels, and spiritual presences are akin to and cooperate with translation experiences.

The most popular biblical account of this occurrence relates Philip's supernatural encounter with the Ethiopian eunuch. This encounter began both with the voice of the angel of the Lord and the voice of the Spirit of the Lord. The angel audibly *spoke unto Philip* instructing him to "Go down to Gaza," (Acts 8:26); and then the Holy Spirit *said unto Philip,* "Go near and join thyself to this chariot," (Acts 8:29).

Whether it is in an *out-of-body experience* (when the spirit leaves the body and travels while the body stays in place), or an experience of supernatural *translation* (when the body travels, invisibly, with the spirit), the normal process, for the most part, involves a sort of revelation from the Lord instructing the person throughout the experience. These kinds of experiences need to be directly initiated and strictly monitored by God, so there is no doubt He will clearly speak and show us things when translation occurs. This way we will only travel where He wants us to go and not where we may want to go. In spiritual travel, the Prophet Ezekiel went where the Lord told him to go, and saw what the Lord told him to see: "The Lord said, 'Go in, and see...' So I went in, and saw," (Ezekiel 8:9-10).

12: Heavenly Visitation

There are three heavens which the Bible describes: our earth's immediate atmosphere, outer space, and the Paradise of God, (this is also known as the Third Heaven; 2Corinthians 12:2-4). A *heavenly visitation* vision is specifically one in which the person temporarily visits the Third Heaven in an *out-at-body experience* that involves a kind of "Come up Hither" from the Lord.

In this type of vision, the person's spirit is brought upward past the first, lower heaven, then past the second, stellar heaven, and approaches the Third, highest Heaven, which is the paradisal Abode of God. This can occur in answer to prayer but, as with most visions, it must be directly ordered and initiated by God.

Paradise is a very great and large place. When summoned up There by the Lord, any amount of revelation can be disclosed, and any amount of scenery can be seen, depending on what the Lord would have us to behold. Some people who have had a heavenly visitation have only partially approached the Gates of that Great City before they were drawn back down to earth, sometimes in only a matter of moments. Others have been invited to come in and enter those gates and enjoy converse and fellowship with some of the saints and angels which are there, and even to meet Jesus. Some are shown much, some are shown little. Most, however, return with a ringing testimony of the glories which await God's people who are faithful to Him. Many People who have visited Heaven have returned with new anointings and powerful messages attesting to the reality of the Kingdom of God.

As it is with most supernatural experiences, the *heavenly visitation* vision can begin with a lesser kind of vision. When John had a heavenly visitation while on Patmos Island, it was a gradual supernatural experience. First he heard the *audible voice* of Jesus, (Revelation 1:10); when he yielded to that, he beheld an *open heaven* and a *divine sight,* (1:12); then he went into a *trance,* (1:17); and then the divine summons "Come up Hither, and I will show you things..." was given him, (4:1-2).

We should learn how to yield to the manifestations of Holy Spirit from one phase to the next because a great vision usually begins with a lesser kind which we must permit if we're going to get to the greater. The beginnings of a great move of God will usually be preceded by a gentle, subtle, indistinct moving of His Spirit. A not-so-spectacular disclosing will, more often than not, precede a spectacular disclosing.

SPECIAL REVELATIONS

A special revelation is when God brings us to a new understanding of Himself or of His Word—an understanding which we didn't have before and were having trouble arriving at. The Apostle Peter's trance on the housetop (Acts 10:9-16), was given for the purpose of enlightening him to a more full sense of the Great Commission, a sense of it which his natural thinking wouldn't receive well by itself. Jesus brought him "up hither" to a more perfect understanding in a special revelation which came via a supernatural trance.

Acts 10:15 What God hath cleansed, that call not thou common.

Before His resurrection from the dead, Jesus' ministry was limited to Israel. After His resurrection, and the inception of the Age of Grace with the descent of the Spirit, a number of things changed. The Gospel was to be published throughout the whole world. It took a supernatural trance with a current, fresh revelation from Heaven, for Peter to get it. Likewise today, Christians may be doing the "work of the Lord" with complete sincerity and passion, but may not be reaching certain spaces because they have defined as "unclean" some things—and some communities—that God has made "clean." Mid-last century, television was considered to be of the devil, and eventually so was the Internet. Some, today, still consider hanging out with celebrities and worldly folks forbidden, but God calls them treasures for whom Christ died.

Linear models of life-paths are no longer. Unconvention is the new model. God's servants are in all colors, shapes, and styles. Karla, a Goth girl at The Katharine Gibbs School, who happens to be Catholic, is one of the sweetest and most angelic individuals I have ever met. As I stated in Chapter 1, referring to Romans 14, nothing is unclean of itself; all things indeed are pure. And who are we to judge Jesus' servants? Let us follow after the things that make for peace, and things wherewith one may edify another. For the Kingdom of God is righteousness and peace and joy in the Holy Ghost.

God has people in every part of the world, in every industry. If we can get a glimpse of the unconventional forms of His plans and processes, it might revolutionize our thinking with regard to what is okay and what is not okay, and with regard to the meaning of "Come out from among them and be ye separate," (2Corinthians 6:17).

Isaiah 55:8-9 For My thoughts are not your thoughts, neither are your ways My ways, saith the Lord. For as the heavens are higher than the earth, so are My ways higher than your ways, and My thoughts than your thoughts.

As I mentioned earlier, we have got to really know the Lord, His ways and His moods, if we are going to be able to discern His leadings. If getting to know Him will require coming away from "sharing the Gospel" with others for a decade and simply hanging out with Him (so we can become transformed by His heart), then so be it. He is far beyond what we give Him credit for, and His parameters are also not limited to ours.

In Genesis 2:20, Adam received a special revelation concerning man's need for a woman. God wrought in this instance not in a supernatural way; He allowed Adam to perceive with his eyes and figure out with his own mind his need for a woman. He saw the animals operate as male and female, produce families, and entertain each other. This caused Adam to have a desire which God did afterwards fulfill.

The Bereans, in Acts 17:10-12, were a very noble sort of folk. They searched the Scriptures sincerely seeking the truth. So God brought them into a more perfect understanding of the Word by special revelation of the Word of God through Paul's ministry. The mind of these Bereans was ready and open to true revelations and rightly dividing of the Word of Truth. Therefore God didn't have to stun them supernaturally with a trance or a spectacular visit by an angel to get their attention. Of course He could have if He wanted to, but God works not the same way in each case. Each individual case is uniquely different—be it supernatural or be it through the Word, be it through natural wisdom or be it through some other means of communication.

In this message about how God speaks in visions, we haved skipped from Genesis to Revelation and picked out certain figures, biblical examples of persons who have experienced a special revelation from God. These are model illustrations of true revelations of God. If our experience doesn't follow exactly as the biblical records, yet the Spirit behind our experience must coincide with and give the same testimony as those in the written Word of God; these are given and handed down to us for examples, (Philippians 3:17).

In this season of revival, we will have a greater outpouring of the Spirit of God than ever before, therefore greater experiences. The Bible examples serve as the base from which God will launch that which He will manifest in fullness through us before the Second Advent of the Lord.

Needful to say also is that we are to reject any revelation, any supernatural experience, or any teaching that contradicts or in any way tends to lead us away from God's written Word, the Holy Bible. Deceivers are multiplying in the world (Matthew 24:4-5) introducing doctrines of demons (1Timothy 4:1-2), and they are to be rejected, (Galatians 1:6-9).

For a more thorough elaboration of the topic of spiritual discernment, read *Try the Dreams Whether they are of God,* which is Chapter 6 of *Understanding Supernatural Dreams According to the Bible, A Living Classic,* offered below.

God is giving us in this season spiritual discernment as never before. We are to know them who labor among us in spirit and in truth (even when their walk with God and ministry style differs from ours); and God will confirm His unadulterated Holy Word with signs and wonders following (Mark 16:20).

Books by David A. Castro

Understanding Supernatural Dreams According to the Bible
A Living Classic, $24.95

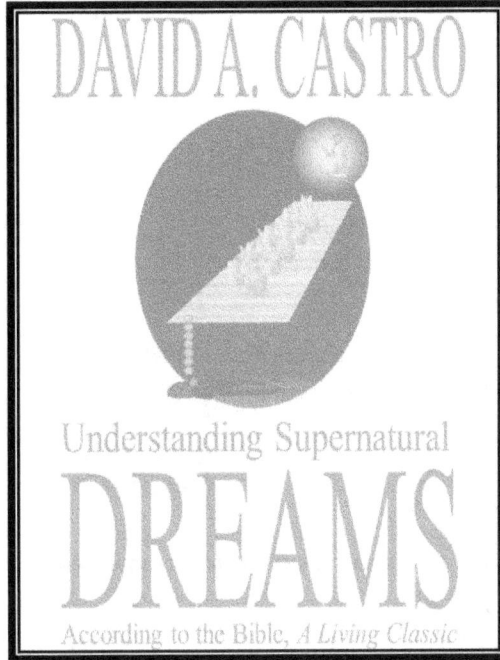

A profoundly spiritual, strictly biblical work, this expository reference book may be considered "required reading" for students of the Spirit. It takes the reader on into the spiritual realm and examines dreams therefrom. A classic in its field, it offers to help the reader understand the broad spectrum of dreams and dreaming, and may assist in healing and deliverance from sleep/dream problems. It provides many practical guidelines on trances, audible voices, out-of-body experiences, and other kinds of visions, and encourages the Body of Christ to yield to the Holy Spirit for supernatural experiences along these lines. Highly Recommended.

Chapters include: What is a Dream?; Be Renewed in the Spirit of Your Dream Life; Sleep in Heavenly Peace; Adventures in the Night Seasons; Dream Recall and Interpretation; Try the Dreams Whether they are of God; Some Experiences; Supernatural Dreams and Trances; Endtime Dreamers; Glossary; 254 pages; 8¼ x 10½"

Understanding Supernatural Visions According to the Bible
$19.95

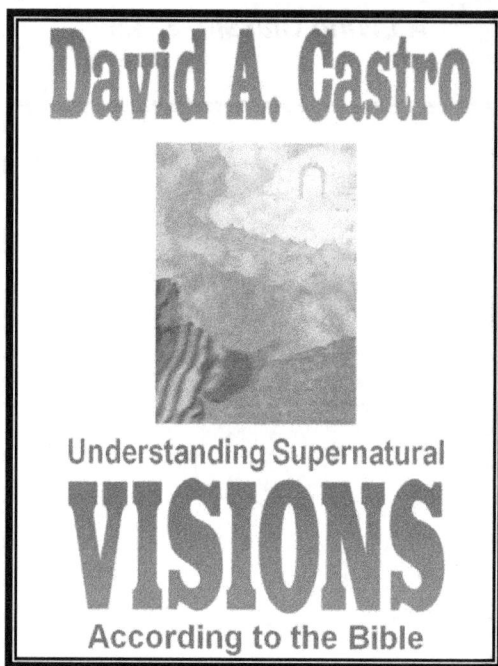

Explores a variety of different kinds of visions and clarifies many issues involved in the various realms of supernatural revelations. It encourages Christians to seek those things which are Above (Colossians 3:1), while at the same time challenges us to gain a foundation in the Word of God, to check the motives of our own hearts, and to walk in the anointing of the Holy Spirit with Jesus. It is profoundly insightful and helpful to prophets, intercessors, and others who receive visions and revelations of the Lord.

Chapters include: Spiritual Vision; Pictorial Vision; Panoramic Vision; Dream (Night Vision); Audible Message; Apparition; Divine Sight; Open Heaven; Trance; Out-of-body Experience; Translation; Heavenly Visitation; Wisdom is the Principal Thing; Glossary; 100 pages; 8¼ x 10½"

Understanding Voices, Noises & Presences
in the Spiritual Realm, $14.95

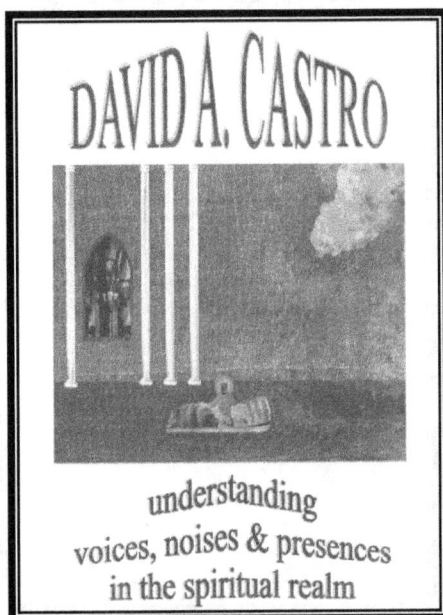

In this unique booklet, David addresses spiritual and mystical experiences in a refreshingly insightful manner. As always, he teaches strictly from the Bible as he shines new light on the subject of the spiritual realm and its various manifestations. He shows how to discern which experiences are of God, and endeavors to remove fear and impart faith for supernatural experiences which are of Him.

Chapters include: Yield to the Spirit; Peculiar Disclosings; Angelic Involvement; Spiritual Presences Around People; Spiritual Presences in Certain Places; Portals, Pathways and Structures; Ask Wisdom; Prayers; 74 pages; 7 x 10"

The Supernatural Ministry of Angels
$14.95

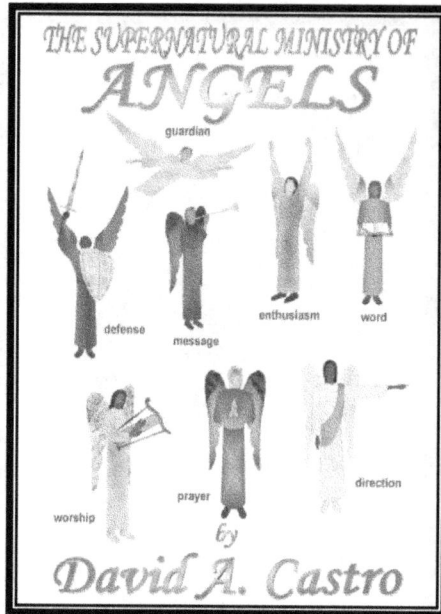

A thorough yet concise study on the ministry of angels according to the Bible. No mythical, fancy ideas or popular notions are given, but a truly scriptural observation and general analysis of the entire spectrum of angels. 30 questions about angels and their personal, practical involvement in our lives are answered, and where the Scripture is silent or unclear, qualified opinion is given.

Chapters include: A Prophecy; Kinds of Angels; Jesus, Lord of Angels; Angelic Fellow-Servants; Angels Unawares; Angelic Providence; Evil Angels; Serving God Releases Angels; Tongues of Angels; 30 Questions & Answers; includes a General Listing of Angelic Orders and Employments; 74 pages; 7 x 10"

Understanding Supernatural Experiences According to the Bible
$24.95

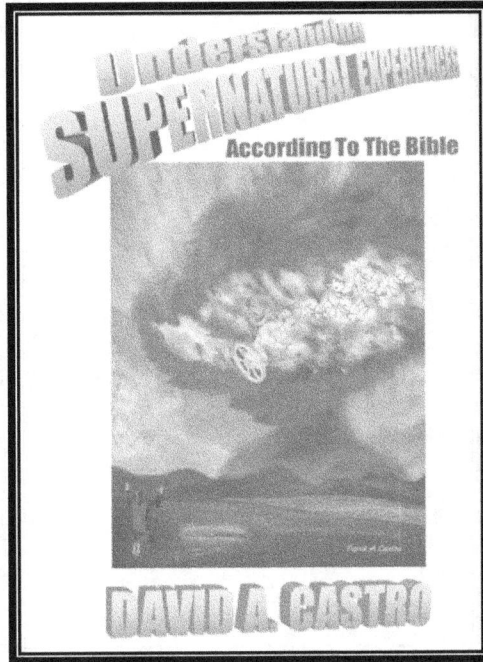

Over twenty years in the making, this extraordinary writing reveals how the supernatural realm works, what the Holy Spirit is able to do, and encourages God's people to embrace the supernatural dimensions of the anointing. Signs and wonders in the heavens and in the earth—revival, special anointings and the Shekinah Glory, trances, stigmata and levitation—are all explained.

Chapters include: Seek the Things Above; My Personal Testimony; The Power of Revelations; Now Concerning Supernaturals; Kinds of Supernatural Experiences; Special Anointings; Understanding the Anointing; Judging Supernatural Experiences; History of Signs and Wonders; Prepare Ye the Way of the Lord; 184 pages; 8¼ x 10½"

30 Years of Dreams Visions Trances
$14.95

30 YEARS
Of DREAMS VISIONS TRANCES

David A. Castro

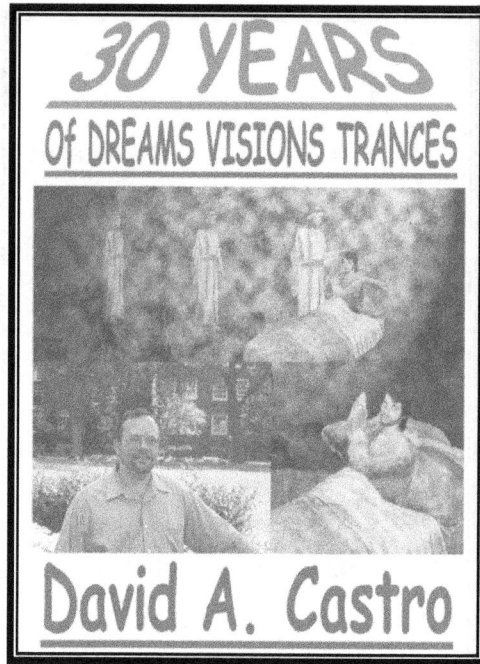

Here David shares a number of supernatural experiences that he has had from the time of his conversion in 1979, in Honolulu, Hawaii. In a wide range of dreams, visions, trances, angelic encounters, and manifestations of the voice of God, he has come to understand their dynamic functions, and hopes to impart wisdom and anointing to the reader through the sharing of the experiences.

Chapters include: Shekinah Glory; Family History; How I Became Christian; I Want to Serve God; How God Speaks in Visions; 74 pages; 7 x 10"

30 YEARS OF DREAMS VISIONS TRANCES

Please order online from www.Amazon.com

Qty	Order Form Sample		
	Title	Each	Price
	Understanding Supernatural Dreams According to the Bible, *A Living Classic*	$24.95	
	Understanding Supernatural Visions According to the Bible	$19.95	
	Understanding Voices, Noises & Presences in the Spiritual Realm	$14.95	
	The Supernatural Ministry of Angels	$14.95	
	Understanding Supernatural Experiences According to the Bible	$24.95	
	30 Years of Dreams Visions Trances	$14.95	
		SubTotal	
		S & H	
		Total	

30 YEARS OF DREAMS VISIONS TRANCES

ഇ ൭

www.brooklynblessing.com

www.twitter.com/daword